An introduction to th

For psychotherapists and counsellors in training some of the practices associated with the therapeutic relationship can be mystifying – and none more so than the concept of the therapeutic frame. In *An Introduction to the Therapeutic Frame*, Anne Gray clarifies the concept for the student and shows how the frame – the way of working set out in the first meeting between therapist and client – contains and protects the therapeutic relationship.

The author argues that careful attention to detail, from first contact through to the ending of the relationship, can make case management within the frame more effective for both client and therapist. Each chapter is devoted to particular aspects of management which the trainee often finds difficult, such as first meetings, letters and telephone calls, money matters, and ending and evaluation. Anne Gray has practical advice on how to handle these situations, supported throughout with well-chosen case material. She brings the scene alive for the reader and also shows clearly how the underlying theory can work in practice.

Anne Gray is a psychotherapist in private practice and a lecturer at the University of Hertfordshire.

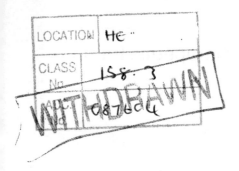

An introduction to the therapeutic frame

Anne Gray

Routledge
Taylor & Francis Group

LONDON AND NEW YORK

First published 1994 by Routledge
27 Church Road, Hove, East Sussex BN3 2FA

Simultaneously published in the USA and Canada
by Routledge
270 Madison Avenue, New York NY 10016

Reprinted 1997, 1999, 2000, 2002, 2005 and 2007

*Routledge is an imprint of the Taylor & Francis Group, an Informa
business*

© 1994 Anne Gray

Typeset in Times by LaserScript, Mitcham, Surrey
Printed and bound in Great Britain by
Biddles Ltd, King's Lynn, Norfolk

This publication has been produced with paper manufactured to strict
environmental standards and with pulp derived from sustainable forests.

British Library Cataloguing in Publication Data
A catalogue record for this book is available from the British Library

Library of Congress Cataloging in Publication Data
A catalog record for this book has been requested

ISBN 978–0–415–10042–7 (pbk)

Contents

Acknowledgements

The experience of working with Anthony Cantle, Oliver Williams and Maureen Gledhill has been influential in helping me to formulate my ideas about both theory and practice. It is to Maureen in particular that I owe my understanding of the importance of the frame, but of course the way I have interpreted this understanding is my own. Peter Berry continues to provide me with support in my work and helped me to think about 'rules'. I am grateful to Edwina Welham for her encouragement and sensitively timed advice. My own experience of the therapeutic relationship underlies all that I have written, as well as continuing to enrich every aspect of my life. My family, my husband in particular, has provided me with an invaluable source of down-to-earth critical evaluation, as well as good humoured support in times of stress. Finally, but most important of all, I want to acknowledge my greatest debt: to the people who have come to me for help with their difficulties.

Introduction

I have been working as a therapist for fifteen years, both in the voluntary and the public sector, first as a counsellor and then as a psychotherapist. I now practise privately, and also teach and supervise students on a university counselling course. When I started my own training, the ideas that guided my work were those of Carl Rogers – the person-centred approach. Then I became interested in psychoanalysis, which led me to the ideas of Freud and other psychoanalytic thinkers, and gradually to the desire to experience analysis myself. Many years later I can begin to see how all these influences inform my work.

The course on which I teach embraces both psychodynamic and person-centred concepts, an unusual combination. Unusual because psychodynamics are concerned with mental processes and the laws that govern mental action, whereas person-centred concepts are concerned with a particular way of being with people, not with trying to understand the unconscious reasons for the way they think or feel as they do. Psychodynamic theories include a whole range of different but inter-relating ideas about the development of the human mind, and central to this is the concept of the unconscious. The underlying assumption is that although we *can* make rational choices, there are also unconscious forces determining our actions. Childhood is seen as fundamental, and present difficulties are understood in the light of past experiences. Carl Rogers, who founded a school of therapy originally known as client-centred counselling, was not concerned with theories of the mind – although he had views about childhood and its influence on later development – but with the here and now of the therapeutic relationship. His ideas belong to a group of therapies coming under the heading of humanistic psychology. These were developed, in the main in America, as a reaction to mechanistic forms of psychology, and also in opposition to the way in which psychoanalysis was being practised. Psychoanalysis is the name given to the theory and practice of a specific therapy, analysis, which is concerned with understanding the unconscious. In the United States the practice of psychoanalysis had become excessively rigid, theory becoming more important than the individual. Rogers sought to place the client at the heart of the process: client-centred counselling. In Great Britain, there is not such a sharp divide between psychodynamic theories (those informed by psychoanalysis and the concept of the unconscious) and the humanistic psychologies, but of course there are differences. We could say that psychoanalysis in particular, and psychodynamic theories in general, emphasize the importance of early influences: whereas therapies coming under the humanistic psychology heading, particularly the person-centred approach, concentrate more on the here and now. This is simplistic, however, as therapists of both schools will be aware of the part played by the past, as well as being aware of the importance of the present.

Perhaps here it is worth stating something that is obvious and yet tends to get lost in arguments about theory, and this is that all practitioners, whatever label they put to their practice, are individuals, and the way in which they behave in their consulting rooms may owe less to theoretical ideas than to the sort of people they are. We all have to discover for ourselves which particular school we wish to follow, what sort of training we want, and how we will work with clients. The way in which the therapeutic relationship is established and maintained is not simply about theory – it is about the experience itself. And it is most likely to be effective when the ideas we hold are not simply intellectual but deeply connected with our emotional lives. My position is this: the way I think about people and their difficulties stems from psychodynamic theories; the way I try to be with people is influenced by person-centred ideas.

I have had to struggle to find this position and of course the struggle goes on. In my teaching role I see students striving to find their own very personal ways of becoming therapists. It is this experience, as well as my own memories of being a student, that led me to write this book. Being constantly challenged to explain why I thought particular practices should be adopted made me acutely aware of how mystifying some of the ideas I was encouraging were. The audience I had in my mind as I tried to formulate my thoughts were trainees, whether counsellors or psychotherapists, although I hope what I have to say will be of interest to more seasoned practitioners. A particular concept underlies all my ideas: the frame. This term refers to the way of working that is set out in the first meeting. I am going to show how the frame can protect the therapeutic relationship and inform the therapist's understanding of the process of therapy. An approach to case management is suggested which pays careful attention to detail: from the first telephone enquiry, the initial consultation, regular sessions, through to the last meeting.

In the casework that is described I have deliberately concentrated on clients who were seen once weekly, and on those who sat in a chair rather than lay on a couch. However, for those who choose an analytic orientation, there is often a requirement that a training case is seen two, three or more times weekly, preferably lying on a couch. Counsellors are more likely to be offering just one session per week and their clients will usually be sitting opposite them in a chair. It is often these factors which give rise to thoughts of superior or inferior rather than of different training, therefore I have preferred to use examples that do not highlight differences. The reality is that some people want more than one session a week, whereas others do not, some want to lie on a couch, while others find the idea terrifying; some can afford two, three or more sessions, others can't. We work with what is possible, with reality and with resistance. Understanding and change can come from a single weekly meeting or from many, from an upright or a prone position – there is no prerequisite determining the outcome.

I have decided to use the words 'therapist' and 'client' to refer to the two participants. Therapist, because it is a generic term and does not suggest a specific form of treatment but simply describes anyone who is concerned with healing. Client, not because I particularly like this term but because the words 'patient' and 'analysand' are usually taken to mean that the treatment described is either psychotherapy or psycho-analysis. All labels are restricting, but necessary if we want to discuss the processes we are engaged in. The term client seems to have been adopted in an attempt to move away from the medical model but whenever a new word is coined, in time, it gathers around it associations which were not intended at its inception. In some ways the word 'patient' is rather apt – because of the connection with suffering and endurance. However, since my aim is not to emphasize differences but to show how a particular way of thinking can illuminate many varying practices, I have decided to use a term which is familiar to all practi-tioners, even if not the one they would use themselves.

When a practitioner decides to write about his or her work with clients, what was private becomes public, so that there is a breach in the privacy envisaged at the inception of the relationships. I thought hard about this issue and considered the possibility of combining case material, but this did not seem right, as it would defeat the object of trying honestly to assess what had happened. I also thought about changing all 'facts' – names, ages, sexes, interests, problems, and so on, but to do this systematically would destroy what were often important factors in current difficulties. I finally decided to alter what were clearly identifying details but to retain what seemed to me to be essential to an understanding of these encounters. This book is a textbook not a novel and yet, when I move out of the realm of ideas and into my consulting room, I am engaged in a narrative, the telling of a story from my point of view. I am consciously selective about what I include, and doubtless unconscious of some of the details that are omitted. Once I am no longer sitting with someone in a room but remembering and trying to write about what happened, I am engaged in recollection – the 'reality' of what went on is lost forever.

It is my hope that in reading about both my ideas and my memories of meetings with some of the people I have tried to help, you will be stimulated to think about the therapeutic process, and perhaps find some ideas to incorporate into your own practice. Sometimes I will suggest phrases that might be used in a particular situation but it is important to point out that these are not meant to be copied. They are included because I think it can be helpful to hear what someone else says, even if after reflection it is not what you would say. It is of course essential to find your own words.

Theory is important but it should be built up gradually alongside practice. Apart from the first two chapters which discuss the theories underpinning the frame, I have therefore tried to introduce only those concepts essential to an understanding of the particular case under discussion. A glossary of terms is included at the back of the book for those who want a more detailed exposition.

Chapter 1

The frame

Throughout this book the concept of a frame is used, and I will begin by discussing what I mean by this term and how this meaning has been reached. Although the idea of a framework for therapy has long been understood, Marion Milner was the first to apply this concept using the metaphor of an artist's frame (Milner 1952). When an artist completes a piece of work, it is usually framed and the choice of frame is important. If a decision is taken not to have a frame then the edge of the canvas will tell us where the imaginative work ends. When a frame is used, then it is this that performs the function of containing, the artistic creation has a boundary. Some artists have experimented with the idea of containment by letting parts of the picture spill over on to or beyond the frame, and it is only then that most of us become aware of its more usual function. A picture that has stayed in my mind is of a man with a chain round his ankle; a real piece of chain with a ball attached to it is fixed on to the painting and dangles down beyond the frame. This serves to remind the viewer that what is seen is a representation of a particular condition man may find himself in. The ball and chain which is attached draws the eye so that attention is focused on the device. We are confronted with a complex set of images: something contained within a frame, the man, and something uncontained, the ball and chain, which keeps him imprisoned. None of the images is real – in the sense of a flesh and blood human being in manacles – and yet the way in which the artist has presented us with his creation shocks us into looking at his picture in a new way. In this example the artist wants us to experience feelings about imprisonment, and the way in which he achieved his effect was by shocking us into thinking about frames, about reality and artistic depictions of reality. It is interesting that most artists prefer to have their work contained and when it is not the effect is disturbing, the eye concentrates more on what is not being contained than what is. Thus we might say that not to have a frame draws attention away from the main body of the creative work and simply functions to remind us that it is aesthetically more pleasing when it is contained.

Now the idea of a frame in terms of artists and their creations cannot be taken wholesale and applied to the therapeutic process. Nevertheless, it is this idea of containing that lies behind the thoughts of having a frame, or framework, for what happens between the therapist and the client. Robert Langs, the American analyst, has written extensively about the therapeutic framework, its importance for containment and how breaks in the frame are accurately perceived by the client, although often ignored by the therapist (Langs 1976; 1978; 1988). He shows how errors are experienced unconsciously, and then through what is talked about in the session cues are given to the therapist to remedy these. David Livingston Smith's book, *Hidden Conversations* (1991), gives a learned account of Langs' contribution, as well as a damning indictment of what both of them see as the established conventions for the practice of psychoanalysis. New ideas are invariably seen as threatening and it is often necessary for their exponents to state them didactically, otherwise they would not get any attention at all. However, the counsel of perfection which is expounded can be daunting to therapists at the beginning of their careers, as well as threatening to those with an already established way of working. My intention in later chapters is to give examples of work using the concept of the frame to understand important aspects of the therapeutic process, and although suggestions are made for what constitutes good practice, more will be learnt from mistakes, from what happened when there were errors or breaks in the frame than accounts of cases where everything went well.

DEFINING THE FRAME

Before we can start to think about the frame we have to decide what its constituent parts are, and to do this I am going to use the concept of rules, which will be discussed further towards the end of this chapter. If we think about an individual contacting a therapist and then arriving for an initial consultation, we can see that at some point in this meeting both parties need to agree on what happens next. Should regular meetings be offered by the therapist and accepted by the client, it is necessary for them both to agree on how the work will be conducted: the framework. The therapist will state the location for the meetings, the duration of each session and the charge made, as well as explaining what happens should the client miss or cancel any appointments. Clearly there is no legal sense in which this agreement can be seen as binding, or any part of it seen as a rule, but unless the basic framework is made clear, muddles, misunderstandings and misconceptions are bound to arise. It may seem difficult at this point to see why such prosaic details should be given so much stress, but I am going to suggest that the framework has connections with the way in which we were cared for in the past. However, I also want to stress its importance in the present, in the here-and-now relationship between therapist and client, where it is essential for there to be congruence between the therapist's words and actions. We all know how confusing it is when people say one thing and do another. We do not know where we are with them. On one level the frame can be seen in terms of a contract, an honest and clearly stated offer of professional help, setting out how the work is to be conducted. In this sense it is similar to any other agreement between two people, whether therapist and client, doctor and patient, or builder and customer. Where it is different is that the agreed way of working is going to be understood as an essential factor in the therapy. Should there be a deviation from what has been agreed then we are going to try to understand what this means to the client, both in the here-and-now relationship and how it may relate to past events. It is important to point out that there is no consensus regarding the frame or which particular elements can be included under this term. However, for the moment I am going to propose that the frame comprises: a private setting in which therapist and client meet; fixed times and duration for the sessions; vacation breaks which are clearly stated by the therapist; a set fee for all sessions reserved; and an internal concept on the part of the therapist that what is talked about is not talked about with anyone outside the therapeutic relationship. I am now going to discuss how the frame is connected with the past and how we might understand what each part of this agreed way of working may mean or represent.

EARLY EXPERIENCES AND THE FRAME

Individuals seeking therapy do so because they have problems in living; these problems have arisen through their experiences of life and the expectation is that the therapist will be able to help them overcome their difficulties. Psychotherapists and counsellors do not have any answers to the problems of living but they do have a body of knowledge regarding the way in which psychological difficulties arise. We might say that through our knowledge of the ways in which human beings are treated in infancy and childhood, we can make predictions about their future development. These predictions will not be exact; there will always be divergence because of the different circumstances that go into the making of each unique human individual, as well as genetic factors which are also part of our inheritance. Psychological understanding is not deductive but observational. We cannot predict or conclude with certainty what we know from one example of human behaviour about another. But we can observe, and the more we begin to understand the motives underlying behaviour the more we understand the action.

We know, both from research and perhaps from remembering our own experiences as children or as parents, that infants require continuity and consistency. The new-born baby enters a confusing world in which initially it is aware of nothing other than the sensations in its own body. Unpleasant sensations such as hunger, pain or loneliness, are modified or eliminated through the care of the mother or mother-substitute. A tiny infant has no concept of time, hunger is not alleviated by an internal sense of lunchtime or teatime, something that will happen when the appointed hour is reached. Nor does a baby have an internal concept of a mother who will come to pick it up in ten minutes, or an hour, or even tomorrow; the longing for contact exists in an eternal present. Slowly, with enough good experiences of a mother who responds, the infant is increasingly able to wait with hope. Baby smiles, gurgles, chuckles and meets with delight the mother, who, in turn, delights in her infant. The baby is learning to give and to receive – it is becoming socialized, the first steps to becoming part of a human society. Of course at times all babies experience frustration, for their needs are not responded to instantaneously, and in this way all of us have had to learn about time, about waiting.

It should be said here that devastating early experiences can result in breakdown later in life, which may result in hospitalization. And although it may be beyond the skills of most therapists to offer help to clients who are severely ill, it is useful to think about some of the factors involved when individuals become unable to look after themselves. If we believe that early experiences can be one of the causes then this can help us to think about all the people we see, since many people fear breakdown even though their fears are never realized.

For those who have never experienced good-enough parenting it may be that they have failed to internalize, to take into themselves, the idea that they are of worth and that their needs are capable of being met. Tiny babies need to be cared for by someone who responds reasonably quickly. If this does not happen despair sets in, trust is destroyed and hope lost. They may survive rather than live, and mental health remains precarious. We all need inside ourselves the sense that we have been loved, and it is this feeling that we can draw on in times of stress. It is often a major life event such as marriage, bereavement, or the birth of a child that triggers memories of the individual's own losses in infancy and childhood. Keeping this in mind can help the therapist to understand both the need for a firm frame, and to appreciate how much the person who feels that they have never had enough care may long for more than the therapy gives. We want to provide a setting in which past failures can be re-experienced so that our clients are able to work through their feelings about these failures. This process is facilitated by an understanding of how past events are connected both with the client's present life and with the specific relationship that is made with the therapist. Moreover through clients' emotional experience of being accepted and understood by the therapist, ego strength is built. In other words, because clients are able to internalize the therapist as someone who is able both to respond to their needs and to contain them, their sense of self becomes stronger.

If we continue to think about mothers and babies we can see that it is the mother who gradually introduces to her child the idea of a containing framework for care. This is not done by explaining to the baby that she will be there when the next hunger pangs strike, or that she is handing over care to father for the day but will be back tomorrow; it is done through actions. The baby experiences over and over again the actions of the mother and it is through these actions that the child builds up its expectations for other relationships. The therapist offers the new client a framework for care which has connections with what the mother provides for her child but is of course not the same. We are therapists not parents.

Without a framework of care the infant may find itself unable to experience its own feelings and emotions. Instead the baby may adapt itself to fit the mother's needs, thus retaining her love but losing a sense of self in the process. There are many motives for wanting children of our own and for those of us who have had difficulties in our own childhoods, one of these may be to assuage deprivations vicariously, by trying to give to others what we felt was lacking in our own past. There is nothing wrong in this, indeed it is an honourable intent, but the problem lies in its subjectivity. We may be filtering everything through our own experiences, a subjective position which will blind us to the needs of the particular individual in our care. Should we work with clients whose difficulties touch closely on our own, we may be in danger of seeing in them the child we once were, rather than the people they are now. The frame provides the holding environment in which individuation (recognizing oneself as separate from the other) can take place. In the best of situations it provides a safe space with secure foundations, one in which clients do not have to manage the therapist's anxieties but are able to develop their own authentic emotional lives. In most societies, in their first few months of life babies are usually cared for by their mothers. If this is not the case then it is generally accepted that constant changes of personnel in the primary care of infants will be detrimental. It is with this knowledge that therapists think about their prospective clients and the arrangements that will provide the optimum setting for the working through of difficulties. We can infer from what we know about infants that we should provide a model of care which is consistent, that continuity is ensured, and, like the feeding pattern which is gradually established, a regular period of time set aside just for the client. Therefore, in the first meeting the therapist states very clearly the arrangements for the therapy. Keeping in mind the idea of continuity and consistency, we say where we will be available, at what time, and for how long. Because we know that interruptions to care are upsetting we also state when breaks will occur due to vacations, and try to give good notice of any cancellations that may become necessary.

THE FRAME AS A PRACTICAL REALITY

We now come to the fee which, although it may have many meanings for both therapist and client, is primarily concerned with the reality of the therapist earning a living. Clients need to know how much they will be charged and what happens should they miss or cancel any appointments that are arranged for them. I am going to suggest that once the initial agreement is made clear and clients know that a specific time is going to be reserved for them then they should be charged for all sessions.

Here I think it is worth pausing for a moment to think about asking the client to pay for missed or cancelled appointments, because it is something that causes great difficulty for both trainees and their clients – and indeed for many more experienced practitioners. What I want to emphasize is that although this arrangement has a symbolic element, representing the mother who is available, it does of course have a much more down-to-earth meaning. The therapist has to earn a living and when part of the working day is set aside for a client then this contract is a serious one. Should we adopt a *laissez-faire* attitude and charge only for those appointments the client decides to keep, then there are consequences for the therapist, and an implicit message is given to the client. The therapist will be in the position of holding open a time that has been reserved for a particular individual and yet will receive no payment. Clients will feel that little importance is attached to whether they come or don't come to their appointments, and of course may wonder whether the therapist knows about the practicalities of life. Of course clients can decide to stop coming whenever they want to and no further charges are made once the therapist is told of this decision. However, if they are expected to keep the time available then even if some appointments are not kept a charge is made. All of us have to find out for ourselves how to manage the arrangements for fees but it is important to recognize that this aspect of the frame, like all the others, is not there simply to serve the interests of the client but is concerned with the therapist as well.

Implicit in the offer of regular meetings is the idea that continuity is important but the fact that there is only a specific time made available may well prove frustrating. Babies do not always want to feed according to schedule. Sometimes they want the breast or the bottle before the appointed time, sometimes they do not want to feed when the mother is ready. Therapy on demand is not normally a possibility and the frustrations experienced because of this may be said to represent the reality principle – the fact that we cannot have all that we desire instantaneously. The reality is that therapists have needs of their own: they have to earn money in order to live; they have interests outside the therapeutic encounter; they have other clients; they need rest and relief – just as parents have needs of their own which may conflict with the needs of an individual child. In the therapeutic situation this will have different meanings for different clients, and the way in which the firmness of the frame – or lack of it – is experienced, becomes an important factor in the work.

We could say then that the offer of regular meetings represents the therapist's willingness to be available (to offer sustenance) to the client during stated times. Unavailability at other times represents the therapist both as frustrating but also as containing. What I mean by this is that the mother who tries always to be available to her baby is attempting the impossible and is not containing the anxiety of having to wait. By not providing sessions on demand therapists demonstrate their belief in clients' ability to manage without them. Asking clients to pay for all the sessions that are reserved underlines the therapist's belief in the importance of regularity, but also leaves clients free to come or not come to meetings, knowing that the time is theirs whatever they decide to do. The therapist is available, like the mother who offers the breast, and accepts that there may be times when it is rejected. The task is to understand the reasons for the rejection. The frame remains firm and is not altered, because this would allow strong feelings to dissipate and will be experienced as an abdication of authority. Should we go along with demands to alter our practice and not understand the feelings behind the demands, we may create the sort of anxiety that is experienced by children who feel that they are able to control their parents. While it may be important for them to rebel, children also need to know that parents are able to withstand attacks on their authority.

Unlike the situation with mother and child, the therapist has to state clearly what the arrangements for care are. But, rather as with the mother, the framework is not going to be talked about in detail; it is going to be experienced directly. It is through observing what the frame means to each individual client, what mental occurrences are associated with which particular actions, that the unconscious can be made conscious. In other words, the therapist provides a setting in which clients can bring into consciousness thoughts and feelings which previously had been outside their awareness. Past experiences can be understood in the immediacy of the present and clients, through firmness and consistency, are able to re-enact and thus understand, in an emotional rather than an intellectual way, how their difficulties are manifested. I am not suggesting that it is through the frame alone that problems are solved. There is a wealth of understanding to be found in the more general discourse that is part of the therapeutic process, but some of the basic realities of life are contained in the frame.

The reality of not being the only person the therapist sees is inferred from the limited time offered; any sense of omnipotence is undermined by the therapist determining the length of sessions; the offer of regular meetings represents the therapist's love; feelings of hate may be experienced through the fee; having to accept that others have needs is manifested in breaks between sessions; limitations of the care provided become apparent through therapist errors; all these realities are there to be worked with and understood. But above all, and most poignantly, is the reality of the passing of time. Each session that draws to its close, every break in the therapeutic relationship, and eventually its ending – all these factors reinforce the painful reality every human being has to accept, that life is finite. The therapeutic relationship becomes the microcosm in which this fact of our existence is faced.

Here a note of caution should be added to what is being suggested. I am arguing that the frame should be seen as a container but it is important to bear in mind that for some it might not be experienced as a safe place, but instead could feel like a prison. Discussing adolescents and anti-social behaviour Winnicott wrote the following:

When a deprivation occurs in terms of a break-up of the home, especially an estrangement between the parents, a very severe thing happens in the child's mental organization. Suddenly his aggressive ideas and impulses become unsafe. I think that what happens is that the child takes over the control that has been lost and becomes identified with the framework, the result being that he loses his own impulsiveness and spontaneity. There is too much anxiety now for experimentation which could result in his coming to terms with his own aggression.

(Winnicott, quoted in Davis and Wallbridge, 1981: 90)

In this instance Winnicott is referring to a specific occurrence in a child's life, the break-up of his family, a tragedy for any child. But what Winnicott is suggesting, quite apart from the obvious upset this disruption causes, is that the child now feels himself responsible for managing all his aggressive impulses, rather than having the containment that hitherto had been provided by a stable environment. I think this idea has implications for the frame. In understanding what the framework for therapy may mean, or represent, it is important to have in mind the individual. What can be experienced as safe and containing for one person, to another may be identified with the internal controls that have had to be instigated when a framework for care has broken down, broken down before the individual was sufficiently mature to master the anxiety associated with aggressive impulses. In this case the frame may be experienced as a cruel and uncompromising structure, a manifestation of the rigid controls that have had to be developed to curb spontaneity. The apparently 'conscientious' or 'good' clients, who seem to manage all the boundaries themselves, may need to be helped to discover that the frame is not intended to prohibit spontaneity, its function being to contain and embrace all feelings. Having made this qualification we can now move on.

CONFIDENTIALITY

So far I have concentrated on the location, times and charges for meetings but there is another vital element in the frame and that is confidentiality. I have suggested that optimum infant care is provided when the baby has one reliable person to respond to its needs; it is this person who helps the infant negotiate the difficult task of having to delay the gratification of its desires. Most mothers are able to cope with the anxieties experienced by their babies by not becoming overwhelmed with anxiety themselves. If they are not able to do this, the ultimate disaster would be that the mother had to relinquish care of her infant and pass it to someone else. Of course most people operate somewhere in between these two extremes, occasionally feeling overwhelmed and having to have a break from the baby but most of the time providing good-enough care. We can see again, if we take the optimum situation, that babies learn best how to cope with the realities of life through the mediation of their mothers. This means that the feelings in both mother and baby stirred up through their affiliation are best contained between the two participants. Third parties called in to help mothers manage their children, help most by helping the mother to have confidence in her own ability to manage her child. Therefore, taking this as our model we can see that what happens in the therapy should be private, anxieties should be contained by the therapist and not become reasons to involve people external to the relationship.

THE ROLE OF THE THERAPIST

In this discussion of the frame I am taking the parent–child relationship as my prototype but of course therapists are not the parents of their clients; we cannot make up for discrepancies in care and we should not attempt to. It may be that in the transference (the way in which past experiences are transferred from the past into the present) we come to represent those who have failed in the past, and through accepting our clients' feelings when this happens we enable them to work through the disappointment and anger that these failures provoke. The paradox inherent in this model lies in the area of understanding and action. Mothers and fathers do of course try to understand their children but day-to-day care requires actions. Therapists, on the other hand, do not act but attempt to comprehend the meanings underlying their clients' manifest experiences. When children misbehave they will be punished, when they are distressed they will be comforted, when they succeed or fail there will be a response – whatever they do there will be a reaction. This is quite different from what happens in the therapeutic relationship, or rather it should be, not in the sense that therapists do not have feelings towards their clients, for of course they do. But should they become involved in actions, whether it is physically comforting someone in distress or refusing to see someone who is aggressive or unpleasant, they will be getting caught up with the past – in the first case trying to make up for what was lacking and in the second re-enacting something that has happened. It is hard not to get drawn into the cycle of action and reaction but if we bear in mind that however much we may desire to, we cannot become the parents our clients may have wanted, we are more likely to help them towards a resolution of their difficulties. Therapists try to adopt a stance whereby they both enter into the client's world through their empathy but also stand outside it through their objectivity.

We might say then that the frame is both like and extremely unlike the care that parents provide for their children. Its similarities have already been stated, its difference is in the prohibition on action. When friends tell us of distressing experiences it is likely that we will take their side, offer advice, put our arms round them should they cry. This is right and proper; it is what friendship is all about. The therapeutic relationship is not the same – we have to contain our feelings in the service of understanding and at times this can feel cruel. However, if we can believe that we are on our clients' side, not in the sense of comforting them or telling them how right they are but in bearing their feelings, then we provide them with an opportunity to experience emotions that have hitherto had to be suppressed. The therapist, through an ability to bear feelings rather than act on them, will be experienced as both frustrating and containing. Similarly, the frame becomes the container for the feelings that are paradoxically caused by it. Without the frame the difficulties that have resulted in the need for help in the first place would only be apparent in the dialogue, the intellectual discourse, rather than taking on an emotional meaning that can first be contained and then understood. Clients often long for therapists to act, to provide concrete evidence of their concern, but by containing these longings we demonstrate three important things. First our recognition that we cannot be all that our clients want us to be; second, our ability to bear their disappointment; and third, our willingness to understand and accept all the feelings that result from the frustration of desire.

FURTHER REASONS FOR THE FRAME

Now although I have tried to show what the frame may represent, I have still not given an adequate account of why it is so important in the practice of psychotherapy and counselling. If we accept that individuals with problems in living need more than an intellectual understanding of their difficulties in order to resolve them, this will give us some clues. It is possible to read case studies in which it seems that a wise analyst able to interpret the transference cures the patient. Countertransference feelings (the therapist's emotional response to the client) are used as a way of monitoring what is going on and as a means to understand what the client may be feeling. Both these aspects of the therapeutic relationship are important but the emphasis is on one person – the therapist – having knowledge and understanding. This understanding is given to the client in the form of an interpretation. Now although it can be helpful to be told that the way in which you are relating to your therapist has connections with the way in which you related to people in your past, this alone will not result in change. Most of us know that what enables us to make alterations in our lives is not intellectual understanding but experience. The therapist provides a setting in which clients can test out responses, responses which hitherto have been thought to be unacceptable. I want to suggest that it is in the frame, the way of working made explicit in the first meeting, more than anything else in therapy, which provides the client with an opportunity to have feelings about another person – the therapist – in the present. The feelings evoked by the frame may have connections with the past but it is an experience that takes place in the present. It is about two human beings struggling to maintain a relationship in the face of love, hate, disappointment and disillusionment. Therapists who use their understanding of the part they have played in provoking these feelings place themselves in an equal relationship. The client's communication is understood in terms of the here and now. At the forefront of therapists' minds should be the idea that something they have said or done has been unhelpful – it may have connections with the past but it is a real experience that is happening in the present.

It is almost inevitable that at some point in the meetings the frame will not be adhered to: we agree to a different time, a different fee, have contact with a third party, are late for an appointment, or go over the stated time. All these things represent breaks in the frame, a divergence from what has been agreed. They are not about the past but about the present. Even if there are no breaks, the very fact the frame is maintained will have meaning. It may be experienced as oppressive or rigid rather than containing. The point I am making is that it is a locus for feelings. What clients talk about in sessions provides us with the raw material for understanding their history. The frame provided by the therapist is a source for feelings to be experienced and understood in the present. If we recall the artist's frame, we can see that breaks result in leakage, and we become concerned with what is spilling out, as it becomes more important than what is left in the frame. The main focus is outside, not inside. In a similar way breaks in the therapeutic frame undermine the primary relationship, and if they are not remedied or understood by the therapist can result in contact being terminated.

RULES

I now want to go on to explore the concept of rules in more detail. Having proposed the constituent parts of the frame that are being given particular attention, and suggested that once stated in the initial consultation this framework for working should remain constant, I am now going to argue a case for flexibility. In his essay, *Two Concepts of Rules*, John Rawls, a philosopher, reminds us that there is an important distinction to be made between justifying a practice and justifying a particular action falling under it (Rawls 1970). It is beyond the scope of this book, and the abilities of its writer, to examine in detail the philosophical arguments underlying this distinction. Nevertheless, although Rawls is talking about transgression of laws and how justice is dispensed, his discussion can inform the way in which we understand the frame. For instance, we might say that abstract rules lose their meaning if they do not take into consideration the human behaviour they sprang from in the first place. Or, a practice which is imposed without regard for the individual, while it may satisfy needs in the person who imposes the rule, will do nothing for the one who suffers its imposition. The sort of rules we are talking about in connection with the frame are rules of practice. We are not concerned with retribution or retaliation when these rules are broken. We do not want to punish our clients when they arrive early, or late, or do not pay their bills on time. We try to understand the meanings behind their actions. The rules being suggested are devised first because they have connections with early experiences, and we believe (I say 'believe' deliberately rather than 'know') these experiences play a part in current difficulties, and second, because they provide client and therapist with a firm containing frame in which the therapeutic work can progress. All we can really say at the moment is that our present knowledge suggests that a relationship in which there are ground rules for the two participants is more likely to be conducive to understanding than one in which there are none.

Our rules are not like laws, where the breaking of them leads to punishment, but are a set of guidelines to regulate our practice. It is also important to say that the frame cannot be maintained in a way that is truly helpful if it is simply understood theoretically: we need to have a real belief, based on our own experiences, of the frame as containing and in the best interests of the therapeutic endeavour. Rather like parents who believe that family life requires boundaries, therapists must discover for themselves the importance of the frame, not simply as an abstract concept. Only when this point is reached can the frame be adhered to without this firmness being experienced as arbitrary or retaliatory. When the frame is breached, whether the breach is instigated by the client or by the therapist, we take a utilitarian view, let bygones be bygones and do not try to punish our clients or ourselves. Our task is to understand what has happened and to base what happens next on guidance by what our clients tell us. In later chapters examples will be given of how this guidance is manifested.

Our rules are not really rules in the true sense of that word, for this would suggest that there is a right way of doing something and therefore also a wrong way. The therapist's internalized code of practice includes a belief based on experience that it is usually best to adopt certain ways of working, which include regularity, consistency and continuity. These are beliefs not incontrovertible facts. We remain open to the possibility that in the light of experience aspects of our ways of working may have to be altered. We remain equally open to the possibility that changing the fee, the time for an appointment, starting a session early, or late, may not be helpful; the alteration may spring from anxieties in the client or in the therapist, anxieties which need to be understood rather than acted upon.

The framework that is established in the initial consultation could be seen as a promise on the part of the therapist. It is a contract, a way of working that has been carefully thought about and put into practice because it has been found, usually, to be the best way of working. We could say that we should always keep our promises even when a particular case would seem to suggest the promise be broken. I think this is true and that generally speaking we should do what we have said we will do. But it is important that each case is taken on its own merits. The therapist should struggle with the particular case and not impose a rule blindly. We must not fall into the trap of justifying a rule simply because in general it has proved right; we must always have in mind the particular individual to which the rule is being applied. We are not concerned with *making* people abide by our rules; our aim is for them to experience our actions, our rules of practice, as containing and helpful to them as individuals.

Most parents try to have the same rules for each of their children, and anyone who is a parent will know the feelings that are unleashed when one child is treated differently from the others. However, most parents also know that they have to treat their children as individuals, and in arriving at family rules for conduct, the wise parent takes a broad view as to how they are interpreted for each child. Perhaps what we need is to have two views: (i) a firm set of general rules which have been built up through experience and are applied to all clients; and (ii) a utilitarian approach to the way in which these rules are applied to individuals. Thus we have the distinction between the justification of a practice and the justification of a particular action falling under it. Our practice, like the healthy society, must always struggle against entropy. If authority, as it has a tendency to do, becomes more concerned with maintaining its own position than with creating a just society, then it will lead to distrust of change, variety and uniqueness. The frame serves the interests of both parties, client and therapist, but it is not written in stone. Indeed there are settings in which the frame is impossible to maintain and yet useful work can still be done. Nevertheless, even in this situation an understanding of what its absence may mean can illuminate the process.

The underlying theory and justification for the frame are now complete only in the sense that I have said all I want to for the moment. There is far more to be understood about this aspect of the therapeutic relationship.

ANXIETY AND CONTAINMENT

Before I end this chapter I want to say something about these two words because they will come up again and again. First anxiety: it will become clear that this term is used rather loosely, sometimes in an everyday sense, the way most of us say we feel anxious in a particular situation, at other times to indicate intense feelings which do not appear to have any obvious cause. To give an adequate account of anxiety, its origins and symptoms, would leave little room for anything else. I am not, therefore, going to address the concept in depth, but instead will take a non-clinical, perhaps almost common-sense view and concentrate on the idea of anxiety stemming from past experiences, experiences which result in fearful expectations of what will happen in new situations in the present.

Anxiety can be triggered by external events, a real danger that threatens our physical person, a punch in the nose, or it can result from an attack on our psyche, a metaphorical kick in the teeth. We all understand these situations and the anxiety that is provoked. The threat is real, in that someone is deliberately trying to hurt us either physically or mentally. However, anxiety also comes from within, from an internalization of past experiences which may have little to do with the reality of the present. In the therapeutic setting therapists adopt a role which is very different from the one most of us would take, in that they do not seek to allay anxiety but try to understand it. This stance is much harder to maintain in practice than in theory and is particularly so when it comes to the framework for therapy. How much easier it is to start a session early, or to give an extra five minutes, or to give clues to what you as therapist expect of your clients, or to act on clues your clients give of what they expect from you; and yet each time this happens a source of anxiety in both client and therapist remains unresolved. Staying with anxiety is hard to do, but when it is done with kindness and with respect it is one of the most fruitful areas for helping people resolve their difficulties. Of course all of us experience this emotion and it would be ridiculous to think that this in itself is a sign that we need psychotherapy or counselling. But for those of us who have had difficulties in our lives requiring expert help, anxiety may be taken as a symptom which, if understood, may help us to see where our dis-ease lies.

We are all familiar with the words 'container' and 'containing': the noun describes an object that is used to put something into, the verb denotes the action. The frame, in a therapeutic sense, contains the interactions between the primary partners, therapist in relationship with client. It provides a boundary between two sorts of reality, that of a more factual or objective outside world, client in relationship with society, and that of the client's subjective inner experience of the exterior world, which is re-enacted in the association with the therapist. Part of the therapeutic task is to understand the connections between these two worlds. By maintaining the frame there is a clear boundary between what is outside, the world of family, of work, of social relations, and what is inside, the therapeutic relationship in which connections and meanings can unfold. The therapist too can act as a container, not by reassurance or avoidance but by remaining open to all the anxieties the client brings. Thus both the frame and the therapist function as containers.

In this chapter I have suggested that the framework for therapy has important connections with early experiences, and that by maintaining a firm frame the therapist provides a container in which client anxieties can gradually be understood. As well as having connections with the past, the frame can also be seen as a practical way of ensuring that both client and therapist know how their work together is to be conducted. Depending on your preference, any deviations from this agreement can be understood by therapists either to make connections with the past, or simply in terms of the present: how the client experiences a therapist who says one thing and does another. I have also drawn attention to the distinction between rules of practice and their application to individual cases. It is this last point which is the most important of all: each person the therapist sees is unique, and our understanding, although it may be guided by theory, should always spring primarily from the personal, from the relationship that is formed between the individual therapist and the individual client.

Chapter 2

Transference, countertransference and interpretation

At first the terms 'transference' and 'countertransference' can be confusing. They refer to concepts that were used specifically in psychoanalysis, and then more generally in those psychotherapeutic and counselling practices which have developed out of psychoanalysis. When the trainee has little practical experience of working with clients these terms tend to be used indiscriminately, and sometimes defensively. The term 'transference' may be used to distance therapists from the intensity of the therapeutic encounter, and the term 'countertransference' as a way of defending against feelings stirred up in us, the therapists, which may be connected with our own difficulties rather than those of our clients. It is important to understand what we mean when we use these terms.

TRANSFERENCE

If we go back to our own beginnings, we will see that all of us develop ways of relating to others based on experiences with those who cared for us in our formative years. This is something that everybody knows but rarely thinks about. Rather like the apple that fell to the ground causing Newton to ask why, Freud noticed that his patients seemed to develop particularly strong feelings towards him, and he too asked the question why. This was the beginning of his understanding of how, in the therapeutic setting, the analyst becomes a figure of overwhelming importance. Not because of any intrinsic wisdom or innate charm on his part but because, Freud realized, feelings previously felt in connection with parents or significant others were being transferred from the past into the present: the transference. Why should this be so? Before I attempt to answer this question it is important to point out that all our relationships have an element of transference in them: into each new meeting both participants bring expectations and assumptions based on previous encounters. However, in most situations, particularly social ones, there is *inter*-action: exchange of opinion, agreement, argument, attraction, flirtation, aggression, repulsion, and so on. In this way, through inter-action, our expectations and assumptions are either confirmed, contradicted or modified. We all know that after meeting someone for the first time we make a decision as to whether we will see that person again. Sometimes, consciously or unconsciously, we decide that we do not want to take the relationship further; on other occasions we seek every opportunity to renew the acquaintance.

If we move from social relations to professional ones we will again see how we bring expectations based on past experiences to these meetings. But now because there is less interaction there will not be so much room for manoeuvre, not so much scope for our assumptions to be altered. Two examples spring to mind: student and tutor, patient and doctor. The student who meets with a tutor will have expectations of that encounter, just as the patient will have expectations of the encounter with the doctor. In both cases the object (tutor or doctor) is seen to possess knowledge that the subject (student or patient) lacks. I am introducing the term 'object' because it is one that is commonly used in psychoanalytic literature, and although most of us think of objects as being things, inanimate things, the word object also refers to people. This situation in which one person seeks something from another involves particular sorts of emotions: most of us feel small and power-less in relation to someone who has something, in these examples knowledge, that we do not think we possess. Because the object has power to determine our future – the tutor to help or hinder in our academic objectives, the doctor to heal our body – we may also feel anxiety. Will they share their knowledge with us, will the power they have over us be exercised in a way that respects our integrity? Thus we might say that certain professional contacts will tend to evoke trans-ference feelings, particularly those which involve a relationship with someone who has knowledge that we do not, or real power to influence our lives for good or ill. In other words, the way in which our parents or caregivers have responded to our needs in the past, will influence the way in which we approach those we perceive as being in positions of authority in relation to us.

It is also generally true that in these sorts of relations the subject knows little about the object. In the examples I have given, the tutor or doctor, the objects, will learn a great deal about their students or patients, the subjects. This is the nature of the relationship but it is not a two-way traffic. Therefore projections (the way we assume people will react to us) although they may be modified the more contact there is, are less likely to be resolved in the way that they are in social situations where the emphasis is on interaction.

If we now move on to the specific relationship of therapist and client we can begin to see how transference feelings will be present even before the first meeting occurs. Clients will bring expectations and assumptions based on their experiences of life that will influence the way in which they perceive the therapist. We can begin to learn about these previous experiences not only in listening to what our clients tell us, but also in noticing how they relate to us, what expectations and assumptions they bring to the encounter. We do not seek to alter these perceptions but rather to try to understand them.

COUNTERTRANSFERENCE

Some of our understanding will come through the feelings we have about our clients, the emotions that are stirred up in us in our affiliation with them: the countertransference. We all know that different people evoke different feelings, and most of us tend to avoid those who stir up unpleasant emotions, and seek the company of those who make us feel good. What is so different in the therapeutic situation is that therapists do not, or rather should not, decide to offer therapy only to those clients who elicit good feelings. They try to use their understanding of the countertransference, the feelings they have about their clients, in the service of all the individuals who seek their expertise. However, since there is a tendency to refer indiscriminately to all the feelings therapists have in their meetings with clients, and label them 'counter-transference', an area of confusion exists, that is as if the client were responsible for all feelings in the therapeutic setting. This confusion is hardly surprising since there is no agreement as to precisely what can be defined as countertransference. Some take it to include everything in the therapist's personality liable to affect the treatment, others see it as only concerning the unconscious processes evoked by the client's trans-ference. It is somewhat reminiscent of what comes first, the chicken or the egg.

If we think about our ordinary everyday encounters we know that we have feelings about the people with whom we come into contact. We find ourselves saying things like this: 'You really irritate me when you keep on agreeing with what I say. Don't you have any opinions of your own?' Or, 'I do enjoy being with you because although we often differ we never seem to fall out over our differences.' Depending on what sort of people we are, the first statement might be thought rather than spoken. However, both statements say as much about the person uttering them as they do of the person at whom they are directed. In the first example we might expect the subject to be upset by our comment; in the second to be flattered by the complimentary nature of our words. Now it is unlikely that any therapist would interpret the countertransference in such subjective terms, but I have used these rather crass examples deliberately to emphasize the danger of using one's own feelings unthinkingly.

SORTING OUT FEELINGS

The countertransference can be a useful guide in learning about clients and how they relate to others but should not be the basis for didactic interpretations. The therapist has to be scrupulously honest in determining who is feeling what and why. A personal experience of therapy will help trainee counsellors or psychotherapists to understand their own defences (the ploys we all adopt to help us manage situations we find difficult) and this self-knowledge, together with supervision from a more experienced practitioner, assists in the sorting out of feelings. But it does require an honest and often a painful recognition to see that some feelings are not countertransference, the client's, but belong to the therapist's own unresolved difficulties.

It seems to me self-evident that no individual, however well analysed, can ever be absolutely certain when interpreting from either the transference or the countertransference that the view arrived at is the right one. Indeed in some ways these terms can confuse rather than clarify. To label feelings as 'transference' can seem to depersonalize deeply felt emotions and are often taken to mean that in some way they are not real. This may not be what was originally intended but it is worth reminding ourselves that the feelings children have about their parents are real, even if they are not accurate in an objective sense: mummies and daddies do appear to be gods, apparently possessing absolute knowledge. Of course in the light of experience this view is gradually modified. In the therapeutic encounter we accept transference feelings, knowing that they will be slowly worked through, enabling clients to see us in a more 'realistic' way. Designating all the therapist's feelings as 'countertransference' can be a way of avoiding the essential task of honestly appraising the therapeutic affiliation. I will now give an example from my own work to illustrate the dangers of being guided by theory, particularly as a defence against feeling.

SHEILA: A MISUSE OF THE COUNTERTRANSFERENCE

Sheila, as I will call her, had been coming to see me for about nine months and during this time I had begun to build up a picture of her world. She was in her mid-forties, both her parents were dead, and she had a successful career although her personal life was not so successful. Her marriage had ended in divorce and since then Sheila had been unable to form close relationships with either men or women, something she desperately wanted to do. It was only after several months of meetings that I learnt of Sheila's younger sister who was living in residential care because of severe learning difficulties. Sheila's father had suffered from depression and her mother, although loving, had been intensely preoccupied in caring for her younger child. When she came to see me Sheila had taken a year out of employment to pursue academic objectives. She wanted help with her difficulties over personal relationships, and with the anxiety she was experiencing when her written work was presented to tutors for assessment.

In the course of hearing about Sheila I had become aware, in the sessions, that she hardly seemed to relate to me at all, as if I was not really there. Often she became extremely upset but never once did I feel she wanted or expected any sort of comfort from me. In fact I was extremely moved by Sheila – my countertransference feelings. I began to think that what was being re-enacted was the situation she had described in childhood when she had to manage on her own, although at this stage I did not want to interpret in this way as I did not yet feel certain my view was correct. The only clue I had that Sheila might want more from me than was revealed in the sessions was the way in which she arrived for her appointments. In the initial consultation I had indicated that I would prefer her not to arrive more than five minutes before the agreed time but in fact she was almost always at least twenty minutes early. As it happened, Sheila's appointment was immediately after my lunch break so that her early arrival did not interrupt a session with another client. When she rang the bell I would let her in and ask her to sit down in the small waiting area.

On the first occasion that this occurred I was somewhat surprised but said nothing. When it happened again and again I became not so much irritated as concerned, concerned that I ought to be understanding what was going on. For some time I was able to remain in this position of not knowing and to contain my anxiety about it. The feeling was not of excluding her, for she seemed to be quite happy to wait. I would read or think or do whatever I wanted to do. I didn't feel anxious, just puzzled.

For a long time I said nothing, but more and more I had the feeling that I ought to be understanding what Sheila's early arrival meant. I came to the conclusion that it must be connected with past experiences, the times when she had to suppress her own need for attention because of the demands made on her parents by her younger sister. I arrived at this interpretation through theory rather than through anything Sheila said. It was also an interpretation that ignored my countertransference feelings. There was no sense of being intruded upon, there was never the feeling that there is with some clients of resentment or distress at being asked to wait. Instead of staying with my feelings and waiting until I understood more, a particular incident occurred which led me to make the interpretation that hitherto had only been a thought.

One day Sheila arrived particularly early. I was upstairs and took longer than usual to answer the ring at the door. She did not appear worried by this and took her seat in the waiting room. But on this occasion I was aware of different feelings, feelings that were in me, for there was nothing to suggest any change in Sheila's attitude. On this day I experienced her arrival as an intrusion and I was annoyed that I could not finish what I had been doing.

The first thing to note is that I could have done whatever I wanted to do. I did not have to feel inhibited by Sheila's presence. It did not mean that I had to be controlled by her. If I was unwilling to go on accepting her early arrival then I could have talked about this with her and accepted the consequences. Instead I started the session with a determination to try to interpret what was happening. In other words, I used interpretation as a defence against feelings, a retaliation for what I felt was an invasion of my time and space.

In the session Sheila began talking about her childhood, how much she had needed her mother and how unavailable she had been. I took this as my cue and said that I thought this might lie behind her need to arrive early and in not talking about it I too, like her mother, was failing to recognize her needs. In the past I suggested she had experienced her need for her mother as greed and now this was coming into her relationship with me. She wanted more than was available and it was these longings that led to her arriving early. Sheila considered this for a moment and said, rather coolly, that it might be so. But although my words appeared to have been accepted intellectually, as a possibility, I was left feeling that she was disappointed and upset.

For the next few weeks Sheila arrived more or less on time and we continued our work, but it seemed as if a gap had opened up. Intellectually she was present but emotionally absent. This of course was a reflection of what had happened inside me. Prior to my interpretation I had been emotionally with Sheila, even if I had not been able to understand intellectually what was going on. When I made my interpretation I had abandoned Sheila emotionally, resorting to intellect and theory as a means of defence. She too was now using intellect to defend against feeling. The irritation I experienced cannot properly be called countertransference, for the feeling was mine, not Sheila's. To say that its source was Sheila is simplistic and involves denial. After all I had accepted her early arrival week after week, and it was quite unreasonable suddenly to interpret what it meant simply because on this occasion it annoyed me.

At the next meeting Sheila was five minutes late and in a state of extreme agitation. The traffic had been bad and she had thought that she was going to miss her session. Suddenly she began to cry but this time her distress was different. I felt involved and so it seemed did she. Sheila said how wounded she had been by my interpretation. Coming to see me, she said, involved a journey through a congested town and she had thought carefully about her departure time. Either she could leave early and be absolutely sure of getting to me on time, or she could leave later which meant she would always run the risk of being late. Sheila said that she knew she could wait in her car until the time for her appointment, but she really loved sitting in the waiting room knowing that I was nearby. She had no wish to be seen early, indeed it was important to her that she came into the consulting room exactly on time, for it made her feel safe. She enjoyed knowing that I was there in the adjoining room. She loved the sound of any movement I made, indications that I was present and would soon be with her. When I had made my interpretation, Sheila told me, she had felt I resented her presence and because of what I said she had thought she must never be early again. Now the thing she dreaded had happened, she was late and the time could never be made up. She felt very angry with me for what I had said. It simply wasn't true, she did not feel greedy, she used the time in the waiting room to compose herself and to think about being with me.

The most important element in this communication from Sheila is the accuracy of her perception of me as someone who resented her presence. This was not a projection – it was real. Her need to be early was connected with the past but not in the way I had interpreted. Much later I was able to understand the meaning more fully, but this was to come from Sheila, and was not a meaning imposed by me. My original interpretation stemmed from the anxiety and resentment in me, not from an understanding of Sheila. Because of the general arrangements I made for consultations I had failed to understand what they meant to a particular individual. It was no concern of Sheila, or indeed of any of the clients I was seeing, that my 'rules' had to be obeyed. It was up to me to say how I preferred to work and then to understand what these arrangements meant to each individual. I knew that if Sheila's appointment had been at any other time, arriving fifteen or twenty minutes before she was due would have meant that I was unable to let her in. But of course she didn't know this and finding that I accepted the time she chose to arrive, naturally she continued to do what felt so good to her. If I had used my experience of how it felt to have her sitting in the waiting room, instead of getting caught up in my own irritation and need to understand, I would not have caused Sheila such distress. Of course it is also true that 'good' came out of my error, in so far as it resulted in Sheila having very real and justifiably angry feelings toward me, but this is not always the case with therapist errors, particularly when they are not recognized.

INTERPRETATION

In my introduction I said that although I use psychodynamic ideas to understand people's difficulties, the person-centred approach influences the way I am with them. On this occasion with Sheila I allowed my theoretical ideas and my need to know to undermine what I felt, and used an interpretation of her behaviour as a means of control. The power of interpretation is an area that gives rise to much criticism, and rightly so. Through the transference therapists become people of great significance in that their words can be both healing and wounding. It was in part a response to the way in which psychoanalysis was being practised that Rogers developed his approach – client-centred counselling. He did not see it as the therapist's task to interpret, and believed that psychoanalysis, because of the emphasis on interpretation, fostered dependency and thus inequality. Rogers argued that transference feelings, although they might come into the relationship formed between client and therapist, were less likely to occur with his approach. However, this position has now been modified and most person-centred practitioners incorporate the concept of transference into their practice, although they are more likely to accept these feelings than to comment on them. It is this acceptance that is so important, and what I failed to do when I made my interpretation to Sheila was simply to accept her.

PSYCHODYNAMIC AND PERSON-CENTRED APPROACHES

At this point I think it may be helpful to make both a distinction and a connection between psychodynamic theories and person-centred approaches. The differences lie in two main areas. First, and most fundamental, is the way in which human development is seen: on the one hand with an emphasis on the unconscious, and on infancy and childhood; and, on the other, with an emphasis on the here and now. Person-centred therapists reject what they see as the determinism inherent in psychodynamic ideas. It is beyond the scope of this book to go into the detail of these differences, but it is important to point out that my stance is informed by psychoanalysis. All the ideas I have discussed in this and the preceding chapter come from my belief that an understanding of very early experiences helps us in the therapeutic endeavour. The second distinction to make is the way in which the relationship formed between the client and therapist is understood. The person-centred approach is to listen and occasionally reflect back to the client the words that are heard. Past experiences may be important but any meanings that may be attached to them are left for the client to discover. Psychodynamic therapists try to understand the past through the relationship that is formed with them in the present, and they will try to formulate this understanding in the form of an interpretation. The contrasts, then, lie first of all in theory – in the different ideas for the way in which the human personality is formed; and second, in practice – in the way in which client and therapist interact.

As I said in the introduction, the person-centred approach is included in a school of therapies described as humanistic psychologies, a title that differentiates these practices from, in particular, behavioural psychology. That the term 'humanistic' is used might be seen to imply that other practices are inhuman, and indeed interpretations that are deliberately designed to humiliate or subjugate are lacking in humanity. Doubtless there have been, and are, therapists who misuse the relationship between them and their clients to encourage dependency through interpretation. However, there are analysts within the psychoanalytic school who also question the role of interpretation. Harold Searles in America, for instance, and Patrick Casement in Great Britain have both drawn attention to the damage that can be experienced by clients whose communications are interpreted with certainty, when a less knowing position might be more appropriate, and more truthful (Searles 1975, Casement 1985).

It is this certainty regarding interpretation, which undoubtedly exists, that has resulted in some therapists rejecting psychoanalysis. And it is important to acknowledge the dangers in psychodynamic theories that are used in a generalized way, so that interpretations spring from intellectual ideas, rather than from the unique relationship that is established between the individual therapist and the individual client. Understandably, when this occurs we will be seen as stereotypical, the source of all the jokes which are made regarding therapists and their obsession with parents and the past. The great advantage of the person-centred approach, using the term in a literal rather than a strictly Rogerian sense, is that it concentrates on the task of simply being with people – something that sounds easy but is in fact extremely hard.

Whatever theoretical school you choose to follow it is important to remember that any comment you make will have an impact on the client. Although the theories underpinning the therapeutic relationship may be complex, the words used in the consulting room should be simple, the language of everyday life. Interpretations, should you make them, and indeed all the therapist's communications, are best spoken in words that anybody would understand, not in the specialized language of theory. If or when an interpretation is made you should be sure of what you are interpreting and why.

The aim of this chapter has been to underline the importance of the transference and to counsel caution in how countertransference feelings are used. I have suggested that any interpretation or comment is carefully thought about before it is put into words. Now that we have some guidelines for practice, in the next chapter I am going to show how we can prepare ourselves for first meetings with new clients.

Chapter 3

The first contact

The aim of the therapeutic relationship is to enable individuals to manage life in ways that are satisfactory to them. It could be seen as similar to the task that parents perform in helping their offspring to become autonomous: the total dependence of infancy gradually moves through the various stages of childhood until adolescence is reached, when, if separation is achieved, the young adult becomes independent. Of course rarely is this process a smooth one, for there are steps forward and steps backward. We all know that sometimes it is easier to tie children's shoelaces rather than allow them to learn how to do it for themselves. But to do things for other people keeps them dependent, and simply avoids the conflict and frustration that arises from helping them towards independence. The therapist's task, rather like the parent who wants the child to learn for itself, is not to give answers but to provide an environment in which frustration and conflict can be tolerated and worked through. This helps people find their own answers so that they no longer need the therapist and are free to get on with their lives.

BEGINNINGS

Keeping the idea of autonomy in mind, in this chapter I am going to discuss the arrangements for first meetings, but before I do so I am going to say something more general about beginnings. This is because, even before the initial approach is made, I think it is helpful to start thinking about the clients who may come to see us.

If we go back to our own beginnings we will find two people, mother and father in union, and then one person contained within the other – baby inside mother. Inside the womb the developing foetus is physically part of the mother, protected from the hostile environment outside until the brutal act of birth expels the new human being from all that is known and familiar. In its first few seconds of life independently of mother the new-born infant is entirely on its own. The painful experience of birth and the terror of that primal scream, in the best of circumstances, are quickly soothed by contact with an external mother. From now on the human infant must rely on a benign presence to help manage all the other terrors that are to come.

Good-enough mothering requires the mother, or mother substitute, not only to feed and care for the infant so that it survives physically, but also to contain and understand infant anxieties, thus enabling emotional development. There is no such thing as a perfect mother, able to protect her child from all negative experiences. Indeed were such a mother possible she would block the infant's mental development, since anxiety (although unpleasant to experience) is vital in that it warns us of danger and helps us to avoid life-threatening situations. But many of us have anxieties connected not so much with real dangers but with an internalization of situations experienced in our childhood that have never been worked through. For example, children who have experienced early separation from a loved caretaker may protect themselves from what has been felt as rejection by never allowing themselves to enter into close and intimate relationships. The child who has felt anger to be unacceptable will suppress angry feelings. All of us want to be loved and to be accepted and the defences we build up over our long years of dependency will include the whole range of human emotions. Some individuals will make themselves liked by compliance, others seek protection with a prickly, hostile attitude, eager to find fault and criticize, preventing them from experiencing love for and thus dependence on another human being. Both are defences resulting in a loss of aspects of self. The ways of defending against frightening feelings are endless. Some defences, however, are vital though others are over-determined, cutting the individual off from enriching experiences – it is these that we seek to understand.

We all know how asking for help generates anxiety, making us feel childlike, powerless and uncertain. It requires us to acknowledge that there are aspects of our lives we neither understand nor seem to have any control over. However long we have been practising it is important to remember this fact and to remain open to these feelings. Of course those offering help experience anxiety too and it is not inappropriate to retain a sense of awe at the magnitude of the task that lies ahead. But therapists have some advantages: they will be familiar with the setting; they will know their way around the building; how long the meeting is going to last; how much it will cost; whether the meetings are open-ended or time-limited. They will also have theoretical knowledge and their own experience of therapy to draw on. Sometimes factual details of the client's history may already be known – through referral letters or telephone calls. Those seeking help will only have their expectations and assumptions to guide them. Having decided to do something about their difficulties, either out of desperation or because someone else has suggested it, contact will be made with a therapist or with an organization. If this is the first time that professional help has been sought, all that individuals have to draw on is their own experience of life and the expectations of others this has given. By keeping in mind what it feels like to be in this position we can begin to open ourselves up to the endless possibilities this encounter contains.

ANXIETY

When two strangers sit in a room together anxiety will also be present. If the strangers share a common language, anxious feelings may be alleviated through verbal communication: introductions, questions, small talk, social chit chat, anything will do. One of our tasks is to manage the anxieties which will be triggered by the new relationship that is about to be formed, so that they can be understood and if necessary modified. To further understanding the therapist must not do what most of us would do in social situations – escape from the uncomfortable feelings through reassurance, questions, or idle chatter. At first this can seem cruel, but by not rushing in to alleviate anxiety we demonstrate our ability to contain. There is a delicate balance, which all therapists have to find for themselves, between letting the anxiety develop and gauging when an intervention is necessary to enable the client to stay in the relationship. But it is never a good idea to say something which ignores the anxiety because it feels unbearable to say nothing.

Let's go back to the image of mother and child, because it is the prototype for all our relationships. This does not exclude fathers, mother-substitutes, relatives, friends, teachers, and all the other significant people in an individual's life, but is simply meant to remind us that for nine months or thereabouts all of us have experienced the most intimate of relationships that is possible. When a woman finds she is pregnant, if it is welcome news she will begin to think about the developing infant and make plans for its birth. When the discovery is an unwelcome one, she may perhaps try to deny the facts and push all thoughts of motherhood from her mind. However, if we take the optimum situation – of looking forward to the new relationship – then this is how we can start thinking about those who come to us for help, not in the sense of turning them into babies, but in the care and foresight we give to the therapeutic endeavour.

THE FRAME

From the very first contact we should have in mind the framework that is going to be established. The reason for this is because the agreement or contract for working together is going to be the container for all the therapeutic work. The constituent parts of the frame, which were discussed in chapter 1, are: the meeting place, the frequency of meetings, their length – both in terms of individual sessions and of overall contact (time-limited or open-ended) – fees, payment for missed appointments, and breaks for vacations. These arrangements will be discussed in the consultation and it is helpful to remember this, particularly if a third party, that is, receptionist or secretary, is dealing with the initial telephone call. As far as possible, receptionists should be encouraged to refer anxieties about this first meeting to the consultation, so that they can be managed by the therapist.

THE FIRST TELEPHONE CALL

I am going to assume that the first contact is made by telephone. I know that counselling agencies do sometimes offer walk-in help, but I have preferred here to concentrate on prearranged appointments made by 'phone. Whether you are working in a private setting or a public one, it is useful to think about what you or your organization say when contact is first made. Clarity is essential as it will set the tone for all subsequent meetings. The aim is to arrange a consultation so that the therapist can hear about client difficulties face to face. If this is borne in mind then lengthy conversations can be avoided, and there is less likelihood of hasty answers being given to questions that need time to be understood.

Some people have lots of queries and go into great detail about their difficulties, as well as wanting to know whether the therapist will be able to help them. These concerns are natural and should be listened to sympathetically, but it is best not to answer questions at this point. A kindly response can contain anxiety; for example, 'I realise how hard things are at the moment and that there are many things you want to know but I think it would be best if we arrange an appointment when we can talk about these together.' Or if it is a receptionist dealing with the initial contact, '... when you can talk about these with the therapist'. There are three main reasons for not answering questions immediately: first, problems cannot be solved over the telephone; second, there is only one way that clients can know whether therapists can help with their difficulties and that is in having the experience of being with them; third, and most important of all, while questions are on one level simply requests for information, they are also about anxiety, and this can only be understood gradually. When you are sitting with your clients and have heard more about their problems, you will be in a better position to understand the meanings behind questions. Reassurance over the telephone will provide instant discharge of anxiety but the client will quickly pick up a way of managing which emphasizes action rather than understanding. It is also important that therapists are honest in their communications and the truth is that although it may feel kinder to reassure, it is not possible to do so. Help cannot be guaranteed and it is better to encourage the client to meet the therapist so that doubts can be discussed. It is through the experience of being with the therapist that the client can begin to know whether or not the relationship is therapeutic.

OFFERING AN APPOINTMENT

Once it is clear that an appointment is wanted, the day and time available for a first consultation should be given. I have found it helpful as a therapist, and when I have acted as receptionist, not to offer numerous alternatives. Experience suggests that a firm offer is more containing than vagueness. The client who is asked, 'What time would you like to come?' may feel worried about the therapist's ability to set clear bound-aries and manage the therapeutic relationship in a professional manner. It is also important for you as therapist not to be coerced into offering a time that is difficult for you. It is better to state clearly what is possible and if clients cannot manage this then it will be more realistic to allow them to seek help elsewhere. Clients should feel that therapists *want* to see them but not that they *need* to see them. This is particularly relevant when you are at the start of your career, as there may be a real need for clients to build up a practice. Nevertheless, although it is difficult to do, it is still better not to be over-accommodating to the client who appears unable to fit in with what you offer. In the past when I have done this, I have almost invariably discovered that there is a resistance which has not been understood, resulting in a failure to engage with the process of therapy, and usually a premature ending. For instance, people who find it hard to make time to see a therapist may feel very uncertain as to whether they really want help. They may be frightened by the idea of talking about their difficulties, of becoming vulnerable, of trusting and becoming emotionally close to someone else. If the resistance – the feelings that are preventing them from making time available – is not understood by the therapist then the contact will be ended.

If I know that I cannot offer regular appointments straight away but am likely to have a vacancy in the foreseeable future, I say so and indicate approximately when this may be, adding that I am able to offer an initial consultation. This is truthful and allows the person the possibility of approaching someone else. Alternatively, the client may wish to take up the offer and use the consultation to decide whether it is possible to wait to see the interviewing therapist or to explore other avenues of help.

Organizations offering psychotherapy or counselling often have long waiting lists, but some offer initial consultations as a holding operation, which can enable clients to wait before regular work commences. If this is the case it is not helpful for secretaries or receptionists (or therapists) to go into long explanations of how the system works. They should simply talk about a first meeting in which all the options can be discussed. Because of the anxiety that waiting provokes, both in the client and in the therapist, it is sometimes thought that clients should always be told in this initial telephone contact if there is to be a break between the first meeting and subsequent sessions. This is debatable since a good consultation in which anxieties are fully addressed can enable clients to be 'held' for considerable periods. To be told over the 'phone, however, that there will be a wait may result in the enquirer giving up. Of course I am not suggesting clients are not told the truth if they ask, but simply making sure that anxieties are not introduced by the therapist or the organization.

STATING A FEE

Many therapists consider it essential to state their fee straight away whether the enquirer asks about payment or not. I prefer to talk about this in the first meeting rather than introduce it myself on the telephone. This may create anxiety in the therapist: what if the person cannot or will not pay the fee? I think this anxiety is best contained rather than discharged into the client. If you are asked how much the consultation will cost then obviously you should answer honestly, but when it is voiced first by the therapist clients may feel the primary concern is with money rather than with them. In private practice I have usually found that people know there will be a fee and that this will be talked about in the consultation.

Should you be working for an organization then it may be that the receptionist does automatically state the charge, and say whether it is negotiable or whether it can be waived altogether. This is inevitable as therapeutic help will probably be subsidized, and the very reason for clients contacting an organization rather than an individual is because they have limited means. Where clients are asked to make contributions toward the work undertaken it is helpful to know what has been said about this by the person taking the call, as it is very muddling if the organization says one thing and the therapist another.

It is important for therapists in private practice to have decided what their position is *vis à vis* the fee and whether the sum charged is negotiable or fixed. If you are willing to negotiate then I think the transaction itself is best left for the face-to-face meeting. Should the enquirer express doubt in the initial telephone contact something like this can be said: 'I appreciate that you have worries about payment but rather than talk about them now I think it would be best to wait until we meet before we settle this matter.' Personally, I think this is preferable even if you are not prepared to alter the charge. It may be that the risk is taken of seeing someone who does not pay your full fee, but money has so many meanings that this transaction is better left to the consultation when these meanings can be better understood. Doubts about payment do not necessarily mean the client cannot or will not pay, but are simply indications of anxiety regarding this transaction. Therapists who negotiate fees over the telephone have cut themselves off from an important aspect of client difficulties. They also provide a model of discharge rather than containment. It is possible to encourage clients to come to the interview without the fee being settled.

CONFIRMING ARRANGEMENTS

Once an appointment has been made, clients should be asked for their name, address and telephone number so that they can be informed if the meeting has to be cancelled for any reason. It is also helpful to send a confirming letter giving details of the time and place for the meeting, as this avoids misunderstandings, particularly in organizations where more than one person may be involved in these arrangements. Although it does not happen so much in private practice, people seeking help in public settings do not always turn up for their appointments. If this should occur, a simple letter acknowledging non-attendance and inviting clients to be in touch again should they want to is good practice. Asking for help is hard enough in itself and resistance may come into operation once the first contact has been made. To find that your unknown therapist is still willing to see you, despite the fact that you have not turned up for the consultation, can assist in overcoming the initial resistance.

Planning and foresight can avoid muddles and misunderstandings, confusions which may prevent the client taking up an offer of regular meetings – or, if our offer is accepted, have consequences for the ongoing work. The aim is to enable the client to meet the therapist. If this is borne in mind then client questions and anxieties should, as far as possible, be referred to that meeting. In this first contact the work of containment begins and the framework, although not yet negotiated, can be inferred from the holding process which is provided. All the people we see are unique. We cannot know what they will be like, but we can prepare ourselves for first meetings by thinking carefully about the arrangements we make for the new relationship.

Chapter 4

First meetings

Having thought about the framework for therapy and how we might begin to think about the client, in this chapter I am going to describe three examples of first meetings. The first two are from private practice, the third took place in a young people's counselling centre. Throughout the descriptions of these encounters I will comment on my reasons for saying what I did or for remaining silent.

JANE: A CONTAINED CONSULTATION

The first client, whom I will call Jane, telephoned in March. I was told that she was a social worker and that her supervisor had suggested she contact me because 'various issues' had come up in her supervision. I explained that I did not have an immediate vacancy for regular meetings, whereupon Jane said she had been given the names of other therapists but as I was first on her list she had hoped to see me. I told her I would have a vacancy in June but there would not be much flexibility regarding the day or time for this appointment. Jane responded by saying that she did not mind having to wait and told me she was able to come at almost any time. I suggested we make a date for an initial consultation when we could discuss matters further. This we did and I took Jane's address and telephone number. She offered no information about the issues that had prompted her to contact me, nor did she ask about my fee. I gave her details of how to find my consulting room and asked her not to be more than five minutes early as I would be unable to let her in before this. It is not ideal to have to ask this of clients since they may have long journeys, which are difficult to arrange so that arrival is precise. In my private practice, although I have a small waiting room, I cannot interrupt a session to let another client in. I have found that asking people not to arrive too early usually works well. Of course there are thoughts and feelings about these arrangements which often come up in subsequent work. In a public setting it is often possible for clients to arrive well before the stated time and wait in a reception area – there will be feelings about this too.

Before I saw Jane the following week I thought about our contact on the telephone and what she had told me. I had a strong sense of containment. She had not wanted to go into details about her difficulties and seemed able to accept the idea of waiting. Her supervisor was known to me and I knew Jane would have thoughts about this. The supervisory relationship is a significant one and the suggestion that the supervisee needs help will have meaning. I was aware too that even this brief telephone contact had made me feel an attachment to Jane. Her desire to see me because I was first on her list made me feel that I wanted to meet this need. I had deliberately arranged the initial consultation at a time when I knew that I would be able to see Jane regularly, albeit three months later. Although this is not always possible, it is helpful as it is likely to be a time that will be convenient for future meetings. It also provides continuity and thus the client will experience the therapist as someone who has taken care to think about her and her needs.

Jane arrived just a few minutes before the appointed time and I asked her to sit down in my waiting room. She did not appear nervous and asking her to wait was not difficult. This is not always the case, but it is important not to start a session early, since this will indicate an inability to deal with anxiety about waiting, as well as setting up a pattern that is hard to alter. It is also inconsistent and unfair to a client to start early on one occasion and be unwilling to do so on others. From the outset the therapist is providing a model of care which emphasizes continuity and consistency.

When I opened the door to invite Jane into the consulting room she came in and I asked her to sit down. She glanced at the couch, looked slowly round the room, chose the chair opposite mine and then started to speak. I was told that in her professional capacity Jane had become aware of many unresolved difficulties of her own. She had thought that revealing these problems would result in her being told to cease working on the mother and child project with which she was involved. In fact her supervisor had encouraged her to continue, whilst also suggesting that a time of her own to talk about her difficulties would benefit Jane personally, and help in her work. Her supervisor, Jane told me, was someone she liked and trusted, and therefore when my name had been given to her first, I was the person she most wanted to see. She said no more about this, nor did I comment on it, but I made an internal note to keep this information in mind, as I thought it might have implications for any relationship we might have in the future.

When a client comes to a therapist with a positive recommendation, particularly if this comes from someone, such as a supervisor, with whom there is a relationship involving authority, it is bound to set up expectations. This is not unhelpful – indeed acting on advice from someone you trust is sensible – but it is useful for the therapist to bear in mind the possibility of clients experiencing conflict if they find their own perceptions do not accord with those of their referrer. It may be that negative feelings will be suppressed, because clients trust someone else's judgement more than they do their own.

Having told me why she had decided to contact me, Jane went on to speak of her past. She talked of a difficult childhood and a very disturbed adolescence. Disruptive behaviour and a refusal to attend school had resulted in numerous visits to a Child Guidance Centre and finally a year's residence in an adolescent unit. School had always been a problem and Jane described a poignant moment when she had stood in the playground and wept at the fact that she was growing up. She felt her tears were not for herself but for her parents who would find the inevitable separation unbearable. Jane later married and had four children of her own. Each pregnancy and birth had been attended by complications of a physical nature. All her children had been difficult to manage, the youngest, still a toddler, having been the hardest. There was a continual theme of physical illness which suggested that emotional difficulties could only be experienced in this concrete way. Jane spoke fluently about herself; there were no tears and yet emotion was not absent, but simply contained. I was struck both by her insight into her problems and by her control.

About half-way through the consultation, Jane told me that she would be moving from the area at the beginning of the next year. She knew that one day she wanted long-term therapy, and that though this was not possible now, she would like to see me as soon as I had a vacancy. She also said that she had become aware in her own work of how emotionally removed she felt from her clients, particularly when their difficulties were similar to her own. She did not know why this was but knew that in other situations, too, she experienced a cut-off, distant feeling. Jane said that she wanted to be able to be closer to people. I chose not to comment on her ambivalence regarding an open-ended relationship with me.

It is important for therapists to accept the truth of what they are told but it is useful to bear in mind that it is not always the whole truth. When

Jane told me that she would like long-term therapy one day but not now, I kept an open mind as to whether this was a factual reality or an expression of her fear of being emotionally close. I also decided not to say anything about Jane's sense of being cut off, apart from noting internally that her containment appeared to be a manifestation of this feeling. I did not think it helpful to make an interpretation until I knew more about her and had firm evidence for my words. I simply accepted that for the moment Jane needed to feel in control of her relationship with me and its duration. I was conscious of the three months she would have to wait before we met again, and did not want to interpret the defences Jane used to protect herself from the hurt she might experience if she allowed herself to feel more directly. It is insensitive to rush in with interpretations, even if they are accurate, particularly when there has to be a break before regular work can commence.

I told Jane that I thought I could help with the difficulties she had described and would be pleased to see her regularly in June. This was accepted. 'I don't mind waiting. In fact I have so much to think about I quite like the idea. I feel better for having talked to you but I do know there are lots of things I want to tell you about in the future.' I was aware of how moved I had been by her story and how much I wanted to see Jane – the waiting to me felt quite difficult. For a moment I considered saying something about this. My impulse had two sources: theoretical knowledge about the feelings involved in waiting and a desire to let Jane know that I wanted to see her. I was able to resist putting words to my thoughts and I think it was important they were contained. It might be that they mirrored Jane's deeper feelings but nothing she had said could confirm this view: to speak solely in terms of the countertransference runs the risk of bringing therapist difficulties into the consultation. Unless clients have said something which you are certain can form the basis for an interpretation, to use what *you* feel as proof of what *they* are feeling is risky. I had been told of a relationship where feelings had become so confused that it was impossible for Jane to experience herself as separate from her mother. She needed to know that I was able to manage my own feelings without getting them muddled up with hers.

I now explained the arrangements for regular appointments (that they would be once weekly and last for fifty minutes), told her when I took my vacations, and said how once she had accepted my offer the time would be reserved for her. I stressed the importance of being sure the time was convenient because I would be asking her to pay for all sessions that were arranged, including any appointments she missed or cancelled. I now told Jane my fee. 'How do you want to be paid?' she asked. I explained that I would give her a bill for this consultation and in future when regular sessions commenced I would give her a monthly account. I noticed how carefully she listened and when I stopped speaking Jane picked up her handbag saying, 'I would like to pay you now.' I noted that she did not like to be in debt, but said nothing and waited while she made out the cheque. I thanked her as she handed me the payment.

Jane sat back in her chair and looked at me for a moment before speaking. 'I feel comfortable with you. I'm looking forward to June but it will be nice to have this to remember and think about.' I smiled and said: 'This meeting has been important to you.' She nodded. I was not asked to elaborate which did not surprise me. Jane had been reflective and this had enabled me to process my own thoughts and feelings. I had not become over-anxious or protective but had been able to wait and contain. Often we feel a pressure to put into words our understanding, and although at times this is necessary, on the other hand if we are able to follow what is being said and process it internally then our clients can have an emotional experience rather than an intellectual one. However, I was allowed to glimpse Jane's anxiety when the interview was coming to a close. She suddenly looked me straight in the eyes and said: 'When I start coming in June will you warn me when it's getting near time to go? I don't like it when it comes as a shock.' I was quite disconcerted and uncertain how to answer in a way that would be both kind and helpful. After a moment's thought, I replied. 'I realize it is important to you but rather than answer now I think it would be best if we talk more about this when you come in June.' Jane smiled broadly. 'That was a sort of test,' she said still looking directly at me. I returned her gaze and said it was time for us to stop and that I looked forward to seeing her again in June.

I thought about this last communication a great deal and when Jane returned in June she told me how important it was that I had not immediately agreed to her request. She knew she felt anxious about endings and wanted to discover whether I felt as she did. The fact that I was able to contain her anxiety and not act on it was one of the ways of Jane finding out whether I would be able to help her. It also enabled her to experience herself as separate from me, something that had been difficult to determine with her mother. In our subsequent work this theme of separateness kept on recurring. And although the positive way in which I had been recommended by Jane's supervisor was at first felt by Jane to be helpful, it became a powerful block in the expression of negative feelings experienced in her relationship with me.

In an initial meeting as well as in subsequent sessions the therapist is constantly engaged in an internal dialogue of processing and understanding. This requires us to make choices about what is said and what is stored away: intuition plays its part but it is helpful if this can combine with an intellectual understanding based on theoretical knowledge and previous experience. In time these two components become integrated so that we are hardly aware they are operating; anxiety is contained thus enabling therapists to think about what is being said and helping them to avoid hasty responses. Jane was in one sense an 'easy' client. She came sure of what she wanted to talk about and needed little help in doing so, but I felt myself to be under constant scrutiny and had to resist the temptation of making clever interpretations as a way of demonstrating my intellectual understanding. Jane was extremely articulate and showed remarkable insight into her difficulties and I had to remember that she was asking for help and therefore needed help. Her insights were intellectual, and what she required was a therapist who could understand her emotionally.

Part of what engaged Jane can be identified in the framework: starting on time, dealing with the details of fees, holidays and responsibility for payment. Learning how to manage these matters helps the therapist to manage other anxieties, such as the unexpected question. When we give ourselves time to talk about practical arrangements we are implicitly inviting clients to have feelings about these matters, feelings that can be expressed if they so wish. If they are left to the end we reveal our own anxiety about the security of the frame. Taking time and not allowing ourselves to be rushed is hard. I have found that making space to talk about the arrangements for future work has helped me to feel comfortable in allowing myself thinking time when faced with other demands. When we are still inexperienced it is hard to appreciate that what is required is not instant answers or outward shows of sympathy and understanding, or indeed reassurance. Too often the details involved in setting up the framework are seen as mere practicalities, trivia which get in the way of more important matters. It is in fact just these details which provide the containing environment that is essential for work to progress. Empathy is of course a prerequisite but it should not be forgotten that sensitivity is also involved when we talk of the arrangements for therapy; we seek to understand how our way of managing the framework is experienced by the client. All of us have feelings about payment, starting on time and ending on time and if we experience therapists as people who leave these details so that there is no room for discussion, we know that they feel as anxious as we do. We owe it to our clients to have learnt how to deal with our own feelings of anxiety if we are to convince them we can manage theirs. This requires us to accept the whole range of feelings involved in every detail of the consultation, not just the telling of the client's story. If we feel confident in our own ability to maintain the frame we can be open to the client's feelings without needing to change our ways of working.

When we alter the framework by beginning a session early or go over the agreed time we are letting the client know that we feel anxious about particular sorts of feeling. Clients who find that the framework is changed to suit them will be worried about the therapist's ability to contain powerful emotions, the very reason for asking for help in the first place.

Let us now look at another first consultation very different from the meeting with Jane and one in which I thought I had lost the client. This example demonstrates how much harder it is to practise than to preach and that however much thinking and planning goes into an initial interview, things can still go wrong.

JOHN: AN INTRUSION OF ANXIETY

A mother contacted me to ask whether I was willing to see her thirteen-year-old son, because he was refusing to go to school or indeed to go out of the home at all unless he was accompanied. Mrs Wright, as I will call her, told me that her son John had many difficulties which had been going on for a long time and which had on one occasion resulted in him going into hospital. She said that she had 'hundreds of psychologist's reports' and would be only too willing to send these if I thought they would be useful. I suggested I see John for an initial consultation and explained how at this stage I would prefer to hear about the difficulties from him. The meeting was arranged and I learnt that Mrs Wright would be bringing her son to the interview herself. I indicated that I would like to see John on his own and this appeared to be accepted. I also checked that if John wanted to see me regularly the time of the first meeting would be convenient for ongoing sessions. I told Mrs Wright my fee, explaining that I would be giving John my bill which could be settled at the next meeting or sent by post. I said that I thought it would be best to do it in this way, since if John wanted to see me on regular basis it would be important for us to be able to work together without anyone else being directly involved. Mrs Wright was sympathetic to this idea and said she understood the need for confidentiality.

In the days before the consultation I thought about my contact with Mrs Wright and how I should manage the interview with John. I had had considerable experience of working with young people but this had been gained in organizational settings – at this time I had not seen someone as young as this in my private practice. The problems involved in keeping work confidential when parents accompanied their children to consultations was familiar. I thought that as I had already set the boundaries with Mrs Wright there would be no difficulties in this first interview, although I suspected that if John wanted regular meetings difficulties might be encountered in the future. I gave particular thought to a parent bringing a child to a private practitioner and imagined that an established agency might seem safer. In this situation the therapist operates within a setting which, by the nature of it being 'public', can seem to give a seal of approval, a safe place where the child will be helped. In a private setting the therapist and the environment are unknown, factors which I thought might make it appear a more dangerous place for a parent to leave a child. It will become clear that these doubts and anxieties of mine intruded into the consultation.

On the dot of time my bell rang, and when I opened the door I saw an anxious youth dressed in school uniform and by his side a pleasant, motherly looking woman. I said hello to John and acknowledged Mrs Wright who immediately said, 'Shall I come in too?' I was nonplussed and puzzled because I thought I had made clear the arrangements for the interview and yet suddenly I was beset with doubts. Was it reasonable to expect Mrs Wright to deliver her child into the hands of a stranger? Did she not have a right to know where he was going, what I was like and what was going to happen? It is not possible to convey in words the intense feelings evoked by this mother's simple question. At the time it seemed the anxiety was mine alone and I was quite unable to process and contain what I was experiencing. I felt panicky and completely undermined. All the practices I had learnt through long experience seemed unreasonable and ridiculous. Because I could not understand the anxiety I acted on it and turned to John: 'Would you like your mother to come in?' He mumbled his assent and the three of us went into my consulting room.

John sat in the chair opposite me, his mother a little further away and slightly to one side. I was still caught up with my own thoughts about what I felt to be my mishandling of the situation in agreeing to a three-way interview. Instead of dealing with this I tried to focus on John. My muddled thinking went approximately like this: I have agreed to something I do not really think is helpful; I am meant to be here for John and therefore I must focus on him. To do this I said, 'John, I wonder if you could tell me about the difficulties you've been having?' Of course what I was really doing was shifting the anxiety away from me and Mrs Wright and putting it into John. The unpleasant feelings I was experiencing were to do with the possibility of conflict between his mother and I, conflict which might result from my attempting to separate her from her son. John was shaking with fear and was quite unable to respond to my invitation to speak; which was hardly surprising since he was being asked to manage all the confused feelings that were flying around the room. The next intervention came from Mrs Wright and colluded with mine by keeping the anxiety in John. She told me how 'worked up' John got, how hard it was to 'settle him at night' and how he would not go to school. She too located the difficulties in John.

It was at this point that I regained my powers of thought and was able to begin processing my feelings. Mrs Wright's description of her son immediately conjured up an image of a baby, an infant so filled with anxiety he could not be soothed. I could imagine how Mrs Wright must feel and it was through this appreciation of a mother's feelings that I began to see what I must do. Mrs Wright was not asking for help herself. It was not my role to interpret what I might think were her difficulties, for I was there to help John. He might or might not want to take up an offer of regular meetings, but that had yet to be discovered. What I needed to do was to exclude Mrs Wright kindly but firmly, to separate her from her son by showing that I was confident in John's ability to manage on his own. I put this into words by saying to Mrs Wright, 'I think it would be helpful, once we have settled that you are willing to bring John to see me, if we could get to know each other on our own. John can then decide whether he would like to see me regularly and can let you know what he has decided at the end of our meeting.' Mrs Wright agreed to this proposal. As she got up to leave she turned and said that in fact she was quite willing to bring John twice a week or more. I said that John and I could discuss this possibility and Mrs Wright then left. I will not describe the rest of our meeting, except to say I made it clear to John that whilst I appreciated the fact that his mother had to be involved, in so far as she would be bringing him to see me, what was said in our meetings would be private.

It is easy to rationalize our mistakes, but perhaps in this case it was important for me to be allowed to see for myself how things were. We can hypothesize about what was going on. Separation anxiety seemed to be the problem although the origin of these anxieties could only be guessed. Mrs Wright wanted her son to go to school. John would not go to school. Mrs Wright felt John would not go to school because he could not manage without her. John also thought he could not manage without his mother. Now if we think in a more general way about mothers and children we will remember that infants experience distress when separated from their mothers. We know too that mothers feel anxious when they are parted from their babies. But adults are usually more able to cope with these emotions. Baby, however, has yet to learn about separateness. The anxiety can become intense, so overwhelming that it has to be got rid of, expelled through projection into mother. Mother can then experience the anxiety so that she knows how baby feels. Through her containment of distress she is able to transform these feelings so that they can be re-experienced by baby but now in a manageable form. We can picture this happening. Baby cries. Mother hears baby crying. She waits a moment and then, recognizing a distressed note in the crying, picks baby up. She soothes her infant, checks he is not hungry, wet or in pain, soothes him again and returns him to the crib. Baby goes to sleep. By speaking gently to her infant, through the rhythmic crooning sounds she makes, by her touch, her kisses and caresses, the mother contains anxiety and communicates her understanding of baby's terrors. The anxiety that has been projected into her is held, it is transformed through the process of containment so that it can be returned but now in a way that enables baby to cope on his own. We might imagine the infant to have inside himself a sense of a mother who can bear distress. It is this image, based on a real experience, which helps the baby slowly to develop his own strengths to cope with the anxieties of separation.

All of us who have had dealings with babies will remember occasions when our soothing presence has calmed a crying infant. We will also remember times when baby has not been soothed and how anxiety levels have risen. Most of us, most of the time, are able to be reasonably good parents, recognizing our children's anxieties and providing a container for them by not becoming over-anxious ourselves. However, if mother hears baby crying and feels his distress as inside herself, rather than residing in the infant, a complicated situation develops. Mother becomes unable to contain the distress she is experiencing, both her baby's and her own, and thus baby now has to cope not only with his own anxieties but also with his mother's. Baby becomes even more distressed, so that mother now sees a desperate infant apparently unable to manage without her. Both experience anxieties, but it is the child who becomes the vehicle for their expression. The infant feels himself to have a mother who cannot manage feelings about separation, and thus mother and child become locked in a relationship in which separation is impossible. Both now see the problem as being the child's – mother because the anxiety is expressed through the child's refusal to leave her, and the child because the anxiety is experienced as residing solely in himself.

PROJECTION AND PROJECTIVE IDENTIFICATION

Projection is the technical term for what all of us do at times with feelings that are too unbearable to experience. We project or get rid of them into another person. It may be that this was what Mrs Wright did with her anxiety. On my doorstep I felt unable to do what I had set out to do, because of a feeling that it was unreasonable and impossible to see John without his mother (Mrs Wright's feelings). Later on in the interview, when I listened to what Mrs Wright was saying, I was able to identify with her as a mother and also to think about what I was feeling so that I could say something helpful to her. If I had understood these feelings on the doorstep, I might have been able to use what I was experiencing (Mrs Wright's feelings) to find words that would have enabled her to separate from John at that point rather than later. This would have been to use the projective identification, that is to understand and speak to the feelings that were being put into me rather than to act as if they were mine. When I said, 'Would you like your mother to come in?' I was indicating to John that I did not feel confident of his ability to be separate from his mother. I might have said something like this to Mrs Wright: 'I appreciate that you'd like to be present but I think it would be easier for John and I to get to know each other on our own. Would that be all right with you?' This would have underlined my understanding that the anxiety being expressed came from Mrs Wright, and not from John. It is also kindly phrased and would have given Mrs Wright the option of insisting she be present, which she had a right to do. The difference in this intervention is that the decision belongs to her rather than to John. It locates the anxiety in mother not child. Both Mrs Wright and John must have experienced me as someone who could not manage difficult feelings. This situation continued in the consulting room, where John found himself with two people, neither of whom could contain anxiety, so that he became the focus for all the unbearable feelings. Once we were on our own I could see that John was extremely anxious himself – which was not surprising since he was in a strange situation that had not so far been managed very well. At least I was now in a position to be clearer about who was feeling what, and could begin to try to help John. The circumstances of this first meeting had many repercussions, to which I will return in later chapters.

ORGANIZATIONAL SETTINGS

To contrast with the two consultations I have just described I am now going to discuss a first meeting which took place in a different sort of setting – a centre specifically for young people experiencing emotional difficulties. Before I do so, it will be helpful to think about the setting and how it can influence the work.

Working for an organization is very different from private practice. There are advantages and disadvantages. The advantages from the client's point of view are that therapeutic help is free or available at low cost and it is more easily accessible to those who do not have sophisticated knowledge of mental health services. In addition, a centre specifically for young people situated in the community is approachable and welcoming. From the therapist's viewpoint, working in this sort of setting means that there are supportive colleagues; supervision may be provided; work is assured; and the organization itself gives a sense of security and containment. There are also disadvantages: ideally therapeutic work involves two people – therapist and client – but in a public setting, however much this primary relationship is protected, intrusions occur. There is more scope for muddle, messages are passed through third parties, confidentiality is harder to ensure, boundaries difficult to maintain, and last, but perhaps most significantly, feelings can be projected by both therapist and client into the organization rather than being worked through together. Nowhere is this more apparent than in negotiations about payment, or paying for missed or cancelled appointments, and in the feelings experienced either in having to wait before regular work can commence, or when there will be a change in therapist. It is all too easy for the therapist to imply that it is the organization that is responsible for these difficulties. Clients may feel relief that their feelings of anger or disappointment do not have to be dealt with in the consulting room. This can result in collusion, whereby both client and therapist avoid the conflict that is part of all relationships and so essential to understand in the therapeutic one. These 'difficult' feelings can be projected so that client and therapist are idealized, leaving the organization to become the bad object. If we remember that the term 'object' can refer either to a person or a thing, and that we all have a tendency to separate good and bad, we can see how it is possible to retain a sense of someone or something as either all good or all bad by projecting (getting rid of) the feelings that interfere with our desired perception. I am suggesting that when a therapist works for an organization it is particularly important to have this concept in mind. This had relevance for my first meeting with a client I will call Wendy.

WENDY: ANXIETY CONTAINED

Wendy telephoned the centre where I was employed and told the receptionist that the psychiatrist she had been seeing had suggested she contact the organization. She said he would be writing a letter of referral. An appointment was made and Wendy was given the date, time and my name as the therapist she would be seeing. It was said that if she was able to, she would be asked to pay a fixed sum for the initial consultation. She was also told that regular payments for ongoing work, if required, would be discussed with the therapist. Wendy told the receptionist that she was unemployed but hoping to find a job. It was noted that she asked a lot of questions and seemed very anxious, particularly about the possibility of finding employment and whether, if she did, a job might clash with the time she was being offered for counselling. The anxiety was handled well by the receptionist, who said that a confirming letter would be sent – Wendy had been worried that she had not heard the details correctly. Her concerns about whether or not counselling would help, and the times of sessions, were referred to the consultation.

Wendy had to wait eight days for her first appointment. Meanwhile a referral letter had been received from her psychiatrist. He had already seen Wendy on an occasional basis over a period of months and said he would continue to see her from time to time. She was 19, and one of four children. Her father had killed himself in a particularly violent manner approximately two years before the referral. His suicide occurred in the home on a day when Wendy was the only other member of the family present. Since this tragic event she had become increasingly depressed and withdrawn. Wendy had left three jobs because of her fear that she had harmed colleagues. Gradually she stopped going out and now had no social life, spending most of her time at home watching television. The psychiatrist had prescribed anti-depressants, which had given some relief, but thought psychotherapy would be more helpful in the long term.

When I read the psychiatrist's letter and the receptionist's notes, I felt concern for this young woman and the terrible tragedy she had experienced. I knew I did not have an immediate vacancy for regular work and that Wendy might have to wait three or four months before this became possible. I also knew that it was likely a colleague would have a space before I would. Then I started to think about the letter and what it told me. Wendy had been to her doctor, who had referred her to the hospital, and now the psychiatrist was referring her on to another agency. If I now passed her on yet again, how was that going to feel? She had suffered a terrible loss in the most dreadful circumstances. Might it not be better for Wendy to wait to see me rather than experience another loss? She had waited two years before seeking help. Did this suggest that now it was urgent, or did it demonstrate ego-strength, indicating the possibility of waiting again so that continuity was ensured? I decided that in all probability I would not talk of her seeing another therapist, but that if it seemed speed was essential this should be considered. I also thought about how much I should suggest Wendy pay for regular sessions. My first impulse was that it should be either a very low amount or nothing, for after all she was unemployed. I was aware too of my own feelings – how difficult it would be to ask Wendy to give anything in view of the tragedy she had experienced. I worked for an organization where therapeutic help was subsidized so that individuals could be seen without payment or for a low fee. Would it be helpful for payment to be waived in Wendy's case? She had told the receptionist of her wish to find a job, the letter had mentioned her isolation, and I thought that waiving any sort of fee might be experienced by Wendy as a vote of no confidence in her ability to change her situation. It might put her in the one-down position – with me seeming the healthy therapist able to dispense largesse and Wendy the damaged individual unable to cope with the real world, someone of whom nothing could be asked. I thought too of the two-year limit that had to be placed on the help offered. How might this be experienced? One fact I missed was what had been reported in the initial telephone conversation – namely that Wendy had asked the receptionist whether counselling would help and had been concerned that if she saw a therapist the time of sessions might make it difficult for her to seek employment (she had been offered a daytime appointment). It is interesting how it is possible to overlook what often turns out to be a crucial factor.

On the day of the consultation the receptionist rang to say that Wendy was waiting. I went down to fetch her, introduced myself and showed her into the consulting room. She was a tall young woman, drably dressed, with lank hair and an awkwardness in her movements. I could see that she was attractive but this was lost in the lack of care in her appearance and in the terrible anxiety that she generated. I invited her to sit down. Wendy sat on the edge of her chair, which she pulled closer to mine, leaning towards me as she did so. She looked very frightened. I waited for a moment to see if she wanted to start the session herself, but when it became obvious that her anxiety was too great I told Wendy that we had fifty minutes together, that I knew she had been referred by Dr Blank, but that I would find it helpful if she could tell me about her difficulties herself.

Many people start to talk about themselves without the therapist needing to say anything at all. If this happens, all well and good, but at some point fairly early on in the consultation I like to make it clear how long the appointment is to last, even if this has been talked about on the telephone. It is difficult to begin talking about yourself if there is uncertainty about how much time you have, and confirmation of the time boundary provides containment. In this instance Wendy would already have received some information regarding the service, as these details were sent with the letter confirming appointments. Nevertheless, it is essential that all clients hear these details from their therapists. This is because there may be strong feelings about the arrangements for therapy, the frame, and time should be allowed for these to be expressed.

Wendy responded to my invitation to speak by saying that she wasn't working full-time, although she did do an evening cleaning job and this was why she was able to see me during the day. She asked if I thought it was a good idea to have counselling at this time as it meant she would be unable to look for a daytime job, something she wanted to do. I felt that I wanted to know more about her difficulties before I addressed this question, so I said we would discuss the possibility of regular appointments and the arrangements for these, but that I thought it would be helpful to hear more about her problems before we did so. I was aware that my response seemed to make Wendy anxious. She gave me a nervous look and then started to tell me about her hospital appointments: how she had been seen by one psychiatrist and then another and how she never knew from one appointment to the next whom she would be seeing. Sometimes the appointments lasted for ten minutes, sometimes longer. The tablets she was taking had helped calm her down but she wondered whether this was really a good thing. She didn't want always to be swallowing pills.

It was at this point that I might have understood Wendy's nervous look. There was conflict about her need for counselling and her desire to get a job. Ambivalence about help and the helper were all contained in her opening statement. When this was not understood, Wendy went on to tell me about confusing situations concerning helpers – she must have been wondering whether this was to be her experience with me. Because I made no intervention that contained her anxieties, Wendy now talked compulsively. She flitted from one subject to another without pausing and I found myself quite overwhelmed by the torrent of words. I heard of a job she had done which involved driving a small transit van. A man riding a bicycle had wobbled and she had to swerve to avoid him. It wasn't a big swerve, she said, but she had become convinced she had

killed the man. 'I know I didn't but I torment myself that I might have.'
I heard how angry she felt with her brother and one of her sisters, and
how after any sort of argument she went over and over the details in her
mind. She had spoken to her mother about these thoughts. Her mother
listened sympathetically but said she should just forget them. 'Should I
put them out of my mind?' This question was addressed to me. 'You've
told me it isn't possible so I don't think it would be much help for me to
say you should,' I replied. 'One of the psychiatrists I saw told me that he
has thoughts like mine and it's best just to accept them as normal and get
on with your life. Perhaps that's what I should do.'

I felt a great desire to reassure Wendy, as the psychiatrist had done,
to link these thoughts with her father's suicide, an event she hadn't yet
referred to, but I knew that this sort of intellectualization of her difficulties was not what was required. Wendy needed time to work her
problems through gradually with someone who could contain her
anxiety until it could be understood. Furthermore, any interpretation of
this nature would be premature as I had no idea yet what lay behind her
fears. It was likely that her father's death had been the trigger for her
current difficulties, but unlikely to be the sole cause.

The constant stream of talk was interspersed with barrages of questions
which made it very difficult to think about or understand what was being
said. I will now move on to a little over half-way through the meeting.
Wendy had been telling me about her brother and how he kept himself aloof
from the rest of the family. She mentioned, almost in passing, her father's
suicide. 'It happened two years ago and the psychiatrist said it must be the
reason for how I feel now. How can it be? You can't just blame things on
the past? My sisters and my mother aren't like I am. There must be
something wrong with me. Do you think counselling will help? Do you
think I'm mad? Can you help me?' Tears were streaming down Wendy's
face and she was crying uncontrollably. 'I don't know why I get so upset. I
don't know what's the matter,' she sobbed. I felt tremendous compassion
and concern but sensed that Wendy herself was quite unaware of any sort
of understanding or sympathy on my part, locked as she seemed to be in a
tormented world of her own.

At one time I would have felt it necessary to say something about a
client's distress, as a way of demonstrating empathy. This is not necessarily wrong but it can be experienced as evidence of the therapist's
discomfort when confronted with the expression of strong emotions. It
is more helpful to convey empathy by staying with distress, rather than
by escaping from this painful emotion through reassurance or by trying
to make things better. It seemed to me that Wendy had had many

experiences of people telling her to put awful things out of her mind, which she couldn't do, so I must simply learn to be with her before I made any interpretation or comment. It was also tempting to say something about her father's suicide, but she had already told me that someone else had made this connection, a link which made no sense to her.

When Wendy's sobs had subsided I decided to talk about regular meetings. This decision was an intuitive one, but having thought about it afterwards I think it was what she needed. 'I can see how terribly upsetting all these feelings are to you and I think it would be helpful if we now talk about you coming to see me on a regular basis.' Wendy responded to this suggestion by saying, 'Do you think it will help?' Usually I try to explore this sort of question but I felt it was important for Wendy to know that there was a possibility of making sense of her thoughts, so I said I thought it would. She became more composed. 'At the beginning,' Wendy said hesitantly, 'you told me you wanted to hear more about me before you would see me regularly. I thought you didn't want to see me, that you didn't like me.' I now understood the nervous look and how my reference to the 'possibility of regular sessions' had been interpreted. I had used the word 'possibility' because I had not wanted Wendy to feel that anything was going to be imposed on her, whereas she had heard it as a get-out clause, a way of rejecting her if she seemed to be too difficult. 'So you came here today thinking you might be unacceptable?' She nodded. 'Well, I'll be pleased to see you at this time but there will be a wait of three or four months, possibly less but not more, before we can start to meet regularly.' 'You mean I would be seeing you, I wouldn't have to see someone else?' 'No,' I said, 'you won't have to see anybody else if you would prefer to wait for me.' 'You don't think I should just put all these thoughts out of my head then?' Wendy asked. 'You've already told me that isn't possible,' I said. 'I thought you'd think I was mad. Do you think I'm mad?' Again I felt the pressure to reassure. 'I wonder what you mean by mad? It sounds as if you have all sorts of frightening thoughts that we don't understand yet, but perhaps by meeting regularly we can begin to.' 'I'm thinking of going on a youth training scheme soon,' Wendy said. 'If I come at this time I may not be able to apply for it.' We discussed this further and I told Wendy that I would not be able to offer her an evening appointment in the foreseeable future but that she could see another therapist who might be able to do so. She did not want this and decided to accept my offer of daytime meetings but was still worried about what would happen if she wanted to do her course. I said that perhaps we could cross that particular bridge if and when we came to it.

Next I introduced the question of payment. I told Wendy that I knew she had been told about the fixed payment for the initial consultation, and as I did so she took the money out of her purse and paid me there and then. I thanked her. When this transaction was over, Wendy told me how important getting back to work was and how she already had an evening job but wanted to do something more interesting than cleaning. I felt her prompt payment indicated a valuing of the help she so badly needed and I was reminded of how important it was to her to find a way out of her present isolation. 'You'll know that I am going to ask you to make regular payments when our work together starts and I've been thinking about what you should pay.' I suggested a modest sum but an amount that would require some effort on Wendy's part, whilst also taking into account the very small wage she received for her part-time cleaning job. 'That's fine,' she said, 'I can manage that. Do I pay you every time?' 'No,' I replied, 'I'll give you a bill at the end of the month. Once we start meeting regularly this time will be kept for you and therefore I will be asking you to pay for all the sessions that are reserved.' 'What do you mean?' asked Wendy. 'I mean that I will be asking you to pay for all the appointments, including any that you cancel or miss.' 'What if you cancel them?' I smiled. 'What do you think should happen then?' 'I don't think it would be very fair if I had to pay when you're away.' 'I wouldn't expect you to do that,' I said. I told Wendy about the vacation breaks and the fact that our meetings could continue over two years but not longer. She asked whether she had to keep on paying during the holidays and I said she did not.

It is always hard to convey the feeling of a session and it may sound as if Wendy was dismayed by the arrangements about payment but this did not seem to be the case. I sensed that what was important was that she was absolutely clear in her own mind about these details. As it was time for our meeting to end, I told Wendy that I would be writing as soon as I had a vacancy and that I looked forward to seeing her again. She got up to go, paused at the door and suddenly shot a volley of questions at me. 'What if I decide to go on the course and have started seeing you? Do you really think you can help me? Should I keep on taking the tranquillizers? Is it a good idea to see you and to keep on seeing the psychiatrist? Would you mind if I did?' I knew it was important to end the session on time and that it wasn't possible to answer all these questions or to understand them immediately, so I said, 'I realize you have lots of things that still worry you but it is time for us to stop now.' Wendy departed and I was left with a great deal of anxiety. Her questions made me feel I had not dealt with issues that were important and I had doubts about whether she would return when I wrote to her offering regular sessions.

I have gone into great detail in this account because it demonstrates the anxiety that can be involved in the arrangements for ongoing work. Wendy's fears were quite uncontained at the beginning of the session, when she clearly wanted to know whether I was going to accept or reject her. With hindsight, it might have been better if I had taken up her initial question and the anxieties behind it, which could have led into talking about meeting regularly straight away. But perhaps Wendy needed me to experience what it felt like to be with her before she could feel the truth behind my willingness to go on seeing her over a longer period. The theme of therapy versus a job came up again and again in our subsequent work and contained all Wendy's ambivalent feelings regarding her relationship with me, the helper. The fact that I ended the session on time without answering all her questions was an important factor in Wendy returning when I wrote to her six weeks later. Paradoxically, although I was left feeling she might not come back because I hadn't answered her questions, it was this containment of Wendy's anxiety which enabled her to return. But of course I didn't know this at the time. I simply had to bear the uncertainty.

In all three of these first meetings the arrangements for ongoing work were an important factor in engaging the client and gave clues to the difficulties Jane, John and Wendy were experiencing. Perhaps the hardest aspect for therapists, particularly in the early stages of their training, is to provide adequate time for a discussion of the arrangements for therapy. We all tend to get caught up in the telling of the client's story or, when an individual has difficulty in speaking, in trying to encourage communication, so that often we find ourselves at the end of the meeting without having settled what happens next. This doesn't necessarily mean that our client will not come back but it is likely that we will get into muddles if we have not been clear about the times for meetings and what happens when an appointment is missed or cancelled. With experience it becomes easier to intervene to talk about ongoing work, so that the therapist is experienced as having the ability to help clients with their difficulties, as someone who wants to see them, and who has thought carefully about how best the work should be conducted.

Chapter 5

Letters and telephone calls

In this chapter I am going to suggest ways in which therapists can manage communications that have to be made by letter or telephone. If we remember that the frame is the container for the process of therapy, then it is clear that anything occurring outside it is not part of that process. This is not to say that contacts or communications external to therapy are wrong in any moral sense, but they will have consequences and we should be aware of this. The aim should be to try to get back to the agreed framework and it is with this in mind that I am going to discuss letters and telephone calls.

I have found it useful to think about these contacts in the following way. All of us have experienced separation from parents and those of us who are parents ourselves will have differing experiences of helping our own children to become independent. When you are a long way away from someone you love, face-to-face communication is impossible and so a 'phone call or letter becomes tremendously important. The words that are spoken or written can be remembered or re-read time and time again; they are imbued with significance, the next best thing to a real presence. Like a loved blanket or the favourite toy to which little children attach so much significance, letters can become transitional objects – unfolded and lovingly read, angrily read, carefully re-folded and saved, or torn into hundreds of pieces and destroyed utterly. Words spoken on the telephone have even more possibilities – they are not subject to any sort of reality principle, and the spoken word can be mis-heard, re-interpreted, completely imagined, or forgotten entirely.

This preamble is not intended to suggest that when we receive letters or 'phone calls from clients, we respond as parents but to remind us how important it is to think carefully about what we say, because our words can mean so much. If we remember the framework then it becomes clearer that the least said in out-of-session communications the better, for the aim is to contain, to bring matters back into the face-to-face meeting. Drawing on experiences of working in both a private and an organizational setting I am going to suggest ways of managing these contacts. To do this I will give examples of the sorts of letters that might be written in some rather standard circumstances. This may appear presumptuous, for after all everyone knows what they want to say and will say it. This was what I used to do when I was unaware of the unconscious clues I was giving when I used words such as 'hope', 'sorry', or 'regret'. I am not suggesting that these words are necessarily inappropriate, for indeed they may convey exactly what we want them to, but we should know when we use them that they express what we feel and are not used with the intention of making the client feel worried or guilty about the therapist. The aim is for clients to become independent of therapists, to become autonomous, not to be burdened with guilt. When we communicate with clients outside sessions we will be trying to maintain the framework by encouraging them to speak to us in the next meeting. The idea is for therapists to be experienced as people who want to see clients, not as people who need clients because of difficulties of their own. The examples I give are simply aids to facilitate thinking. Each letter and each telephone call, just like in-session communications, should be addressed to the individual, but a general format is a useful guide which can then be altered to suit specific circumstances.

SECRETARIES AND RECEPTIONISTS

Therapists working for agencies or organizations are often employed on a part-time basis and therefore clients' out-of-session communications will probably go through a third party. Letters may be opened by a secretary, who will if it seems appropriate leave a response until the therapist is next scheduled to be at work. Or, if urgency is indicated, contact may be made immediately so that the secretary can discover how the therapist wishes to respond. The same applies to telephone calls. In this case it is helpful if whoever takes the call records as accurately as possible what clients have said. For instance, if it is to say they cannot make the next appointment something like this:

> James Smith called at 4.00 p.m. today, Friday 15th February. He said: 'I'm meant to be seeing Mr Jones tomorrow. Can you tell him I can't come.' I thanked him for letting us know and asked if there was any other message. He asked me to make sure you were told. Margaret (receptionist).

This is a clear and simple communication. Of course many aren't, but it is helpful if receptionists are encouraged not to get too involved with clients who have complicated messages to impart. A request for a change of therapist, a different time for an appointment, anything other than a straightforward message about a cancellation is best referred to the face-to-face meeting. This can be done by saying, 'I will let Mr Jones know that you have telephoned but I think it would be best if you talked to him about your request/this matter when next you meet.'

In an organizational setting there are occasions when clients will telephone to say that they no longer wish to see the therapist. In this case receptionists have to use discretion. It can be helpful to ask if there is any other message so that clients can, if they want to, say something about the reasons for their decision. On the other hand, it may feel right simply to accept what is said and leave therapists to decide how they want to deal with the communication.

It seems appropriate here to acknowledge the importance of the many different and difficult tasks that are expected of secretaries and receptionists working for agencies offering therapeutic help. They are the front line, the first people to have contact with the prospective client. The way in which the initial response, and any subsequent one, is experienced becomes a factor in the setting and maintaining of boundaries. Administrative staff have to deal sympathetically with people who are sometimes upset and angry, yet they do not have the rewards the therapist enjoys. Passing on messages from irate or distressed people, without getting too involved, is hard. Whilst it is neither possible nor desirable to turn secretaries or receptionists into therapists, a forum for them to talk about the difficulties they encounter is useful, and perhaps essential. The facilitator of such a meeting can help staff to learn from each other, and the meeting itself can also be used for explaining why particular practices are encouraged or discouraged.

I have already suggested a letter be sent in the event of a client not attending an initial consultation and what I had in mind was something like this:

Dear Ms Smith,

I am sorry that you did not keep your appointment with me on Friday. Please be in touch again should you want to.

Yours sincerely,

This lets clients know that you have registered their non-appearance and that you were sorry not to have seen them but are still willing to do so. It is important clients know that, having missed an appointment, they can make contact again, as they may feel that not having let the therapist know they would not be coming will mean that no further contact can be made. A situation can arise when an individual makes a whole series of first appointments, none of which is kept. When there are long waiting lists and consultations are scarce, this can be very irritating but as far as is humanly possible it is best if this irritation can be contained. There is always resistance and ambivalence about asking for help and some clients need to test out the limits of their acceptability. If the receptionist responds to unkept appointments by saying, 'You have messed us about so much I really wonder whether you want help,' or 'I will have to ask you to make certain you keep this appointment as I will not be able to offer you another one,' this will be experienced as retaliation. What can be done when this occurs is to offer just one time so that the receptionist is not drawn into the client's ambivalence. Let's imagine someone telephoning to make an appointment. They have already missed three prearranged first consultations.

CLIENT: I'd like to make an appointment.

The receptionist asks for the name and remembers the client and the broken meetings. She looks in the appointment book and offers the first vacant slot.

RECEPTIONIST: Ms Barker is able to see you on Wednesday evening at 6.00 p.m.
CLIENT: I'm not sure about that. What other times have you got?
RECEPTIONIST: That's the only time I have available at the moment.
CLIENT: Well I don't really know. You see I need to see someone. I've got so many problems, but that time is hard to make. I usually go to an evening class.

The receptionist may feel sympathetic – why should the client be asked to forgo the evening class? However, the previous contacts suggest that the difficulties in coming to an appointment are more to do with internal resistances than with external factors. She decides to be firm.

RECEPTIONIST: I'm afraid this is all I can offer you at the moment. I wonder whether you might consider coming on Wednesday as it is only a first meeting? You could then talk about the times for regular sessions with the therapist when you meet.

The client will feel that conscious difficulties about making a particular time are acknowledged, but firmness in not offering lots of alternatives addresses the unconscious resistance. The client can now accept or reject the offer. If it is the latter the receptionist can say: 'Perhaps you would like to get in touch again when a different time may be available.'

I want to point out here that it would be quite unreasonable and unhelpful for receptionists to think that they had to repeat someone else's words, but if they are encouraged to think about the client, and what is going on in these contacts, then they can discover their own ways of addressing the difficulties. It isn't necessary either, for the facilitator, to refer to conscious or unconscious motivations, because when receptionists talk about their experiences with clients these factors are clarified. By asking them to stop and consider what is going on, and what would be most helpful to say, it is often possible to explore these motivations without adding to the confusion with language that is unfamiliar.

THERAPISTS

Once an initial consultation has taken place and the client has asked for regular appointments, a letter offering these when they are available should be sent. In private practice there may not be a long gap between the first meeting and subsequent ones. Nevertheless, it can be helpful to send a letter confirming the arrangements as this will avoid misunderstandings and also communicates the therapist's recognition of the importance of the work. I suggest something simple like this:

> Dear Mr Brown,
>
> I am writing to confirm the arrangements we made when we met yesterday. The first of our regular meetings will be on Tuesday 4th May at 2.00 p.m. and from then on at the same time each week.
> I look forward to seeing you again.
>
> Yours sincerely,

The first few meetings are often crucial in the engaging process, the client may still feel very uncertain and therapists have to be aware of resistances and be open to the meanings that may be attached to 'mistakes' on their part. When these are not recognized in the session you may get a telephone call or a letter telling you that your client has decided not to continue the meetings. If I am told this on the telephone, I usually say that I think it would be helpful to talk about this together. I then suggest that the client come to the next appointment so that we can discuss the decision. It may be that it will not be altered. Indeed this should not be the aim, but you will have a chance to understand what has gone wrong. If the client is adamant on the telephone and does not want a meeting then obviously this must be accepted. I always say that I hope contact will be made again should the need arise.

When a decision to stop coming is communicated in a letter, whether this gives reasons or not, the reply should be simple. It is not a good idea to make interpretations in your response. As with the telephone call I use my judgement in deciding whether or not to encourage a meeting to discuss the decision. When you are told plainly that the client does not want to see you any more I think this should be respected. I respond like this:

> Dear Mr Brown,
>
> Thank you for your letter letting me know that you do not want to continue our meetings.
> Please be in touch again at any time should you want to.
>
> Yours sincerely,

When a client has expressed dissatisfaction and gone into some detail, something like this might be said:

> Dear Mr Brown,
>
> Thank you for your letter. I note what you say and appreciate that there are difficulties which have not been understood. I wonder whether you would consider keeping your next appointment so that we can talk about these difficulties together?
> I will keep your time open for you and hope that you will feel able to come.
>
> Yours sincerely,

Telephone calls are much harder to handle, as you have to think on your feet. If you are responding to a message asking you to return a call from a client, at least you have time to consider what you want to say, particularly if the client has indicated the reasons for wanting to speak to you. When the situation is different and the 'phone rings and you find yourself speaking to your client, there isn't time for thought. What is useful to keep in mind is the aim of containment. It is right to listen to whatever clients want to say but as far as possible therapists should try not to let themselves be pressurized into action. Whatever the communication, whether it is a request for a change in time, change in fee, or to tell you about a distressing event that has occurred, these anxieties should be contained until the next meeting. The therapist who is able to convey belief in the importance of talking about difficulties face to face, whilst also accepting the client's out-of-session needs without acting on them, provides containment. This only comes through experience, and for most of us it is necessary to learn gradually. It is inevitable that we will become drawn into out-of-session communications, and probable that we will alter arrangements without prior thought. This is not disastrous, but what is important is that having done so we are aware that there will be consequences.

A client who has persuaded us to change the basic framework of the therapy will have feelings about what has happened and it is useful to have this in mind for the next session. Listen to what your clients say as it may give clues to how they have experienced the change. The rather obvious example is when you find yourself hearing accounts of how unreliable people are: an employer who keeps on agreeing to changes in working practices, a friend who says one thing and does another. This may be an unconscious reference to you. At first it is difficult to appreciate that seemingly reasonable requests for changes are not *necessarily* reasons for alterations having to be made. Giving yourself time to understand what the request means does not have to feel harsh. When I have felt myself being cornered by urgent demands for action or answers, I say something like this: 'I know it's frustrating that I am not answering you straight away but I would like to take a little time to think about what you have asked.' This can be said either on the telephone or in a session. With a 'phone call asking for a change it is quite reasonable to say that you want to think about what has been requested, and if necessary contact the client again when you have given yourself time to think.

I began this chapter with thoughts about children separated from their parents and I have tried to convey how clients can feel contained and held by a therapist who maintains boundaries. Distressed children have difficulty managing their own anxieties, and if parents become overwhelmed themselves by this distress, then their children will lose confidence not only in their parents' ability to cope with separation, but also in their own developing independence. Of course, we are not talking about children, but are concerned with adults. Nevertheless, we all have childlike feelings and it is these, as well as more adult emotions, that come into the therapeutic relationship. When clients leave the consulting room they have to manage life on their own. It is not helpful to get into a situation where therapists believe that clients are unable to cope without them, a feeling which may be conveyed if we allow ourselves to become involved in lengthy discussions outside the sessions. Finally, it must be said that we have to be alert to the fact that crises can and do occur. No theory can be all-embracing and the ideas concerning the framework are no exception. Sometimes we do have to act on a feeling without fully understanding it, and there are times when we may not want to risk leaving things until the next session. No rule should be absolute but when we decide to break a boundary or alter the framework, we can be sure that there will be consequences – positive or negative.

Chapter 6

Third-party communications

The title of this chapter refers to communications concerning the client but made to the therapist through someone else: referrer, professional worker, parent, relative or friend. Much of what was said in the previous chapter pertains but these particular communications deserve thought in their own right.

Theoretically, one of the aspects of the therapeutic relationship that is generally accepted is that of confidentiality but how this operates in practice is open to question and interpretation. Let us start with the ideal – absolute confidentiality: if we believe that this is desirable then everything should be contained between therapist and client. This means that we do not talk about clients to anyone else even if the clients want us to. Perhaps this seems contradictory, but believing in something does not mean that we alter our beliefs because someone else thinks we should, no matter who that person is. I hope it is becoming clear that changing the foundation or framework of our practice has conse-quences, and although altering or shifting the boundaries may result in short-term gratification of needs, ultimately it will be experienced as uncontaining and thus endanger the therapy. It may not always be possible to maintain confidentiality in an absolute sense but it should be remembered that this is what we are aiming for.

Before I go on to discuss some of the issues raised through third-party communications, I must first of all acknowledge my own transgression, because in writing about the people who came to me for help I have breached the rule of confidentiality. There are many situations where the privacy of the relationship between client and therapist is not main-tained: when a case is taken to supervision, when a client is discussed in a clinical meeting, or talked about to a colleague in the same organ-ization, or another one. All these are deviations and they will have consequences. However subtly, however slightly, sharing information about the client will alter the therapeutic relationship. It may be that it is altered positively, through good supervision for instance, or in hearing how other therapists work. Nevertheless, the meeting between therapist and client is no longer entirely private.

In their guidelines, the British Association for Counselling recommend clients be told about supervision arrangements, and that permission is sought before information is shared with anyone else. Personally, I prefer not to talk about supervision to clients as I feel it is an intrusion of my needs, and neither do I talk about confidentiality unless it is raised as an issue of concern by the client. Everyone will work out his or her own code of practice but it is worth considering whether it should be the therapist who introduces the matter of supervision arrangements or of contact with other professionals. People who have tremendous anxieties regarding confidentiality, and who fear that what is talked about will be disclosed to others, need to have these worries understood. It may be they have had upsetting experiences in the past: parents who did not respect their privacy or people with authority over them who revealed information they thought would be kept private. The origins of anxiety may never be discovered if confidentiality is promised before it has been raised as a concern by the client, and an important area of understanding is sealed off. Agreeing to something or promising something is very different from sticking to it and I wonder if it isn't more helpful for therapists to model what they believe – it is actions rather than words that are the issue. I don't mean that the rule of confidentiality should not be observed. Rather, if it is a basic tenet in the therapist's understanding of what constitutes good practice then perhaps it doesn't need talking about. After all most of us consider empathy to be a necessary ingredient for therapy but we don't promise it to our clients so much as try to demonstrate it. It can be salutary to discover that it is often those clients who are most concerned with the possibility of the therapist involving other workers, who then seem to set up situations which invite what they most fear. When this happens, therapists have to hold on very firmly to their own beliefs, sometimes in the face of extreme pressure.

Referral letters or telephone calls from professional colleagues are usually sent with clients' knowledge, although not always. Information that comes in this way is not a breach in confidentiality as the therapeutic relationship has not yet begun. The thoughts of the referrer are helpful and a discussion on the telephone can clarify whether you or your organization are an appropriate source of help. Once the client has been seen for an initial consultation, the framework established and the offer of regular sessions accepted, the therapeutic relationship is made. It is now that difficulties can arise. The person who has made the referral may continue to see the client and if dissatisfaction with the therapy is voiced, the referrer, understandably, may contact the therapist to discuss the problem. It is important to try to contain the feelings that are being stirred up but it is hard to find words that achieve this without talking about the therapy itself. Sometimes something like this can help: 'I'm grateful to you for letting me know about these difficulties and I will think about all you have told me. I appreciate too how worrying things seem to be for Mrs White. I think it's best though if I don't talk about her and her therapy. I hope this doesn't seem unhelpful.' Often a real appreciation of the referrer's anxieties are sufficient and of course it must be remembered that these feelings are being evoked by the client. Usually I have found a comment such as 'I hope this doesn't seem unhelpful' allows other workers to talk about their own belief in the importance of privacy. None the less, it must be added that there are times when all our skill and tact does not result in a good outcome. We are sometimes seen as unhelpful, obtuse and unnecessarily secretive. This was how I felt in the next case, feelings I found hard to contain.

MARY: STAYING SILENT

The client, I will call Mary, was 21 when I saw her. She had been referred by a psychiatric social worker who was unable to continue her work with the client. Mary was living in a hostel with her two young children, both under five, and there was a long history of involvement with the social services. In our first meeting Mary told me more about herself factually than in all the rest of our contact, which lasted for two years. I heard of an extremely sad childhood, long periods in care, and several episodes of complete withdrawal causing extreme anxiety to those who came into contact with Mary. At one time she did not speak for over a year, which resulted in her being taken into psychiatric care. Her own children had been fostered on the occasions when Mary felt unable to look after them herself. There was a constant theme of people trying to make her speak, anger and frustration when she didn't, followed by workers giving up and passing Mary on to other agencies. She said that she suffered from panic attacks. It was not clear what triggered these feelings but there was some suggestion that they occurred when Mary felt other people were expecting something of her or when she was being asked to explain herself.

With the support of my own supervision I was able to contain and hold the extreme anxiety this case provoked; the hardest pressures to withstand came from other professionals wanting to discuss Mary and her problems. A housing officer wanted me to write a report on my work, which it was suggested might result in Mary being found accommodation. I was told that Mary had agreed to this request. I am sure she had but it had not been raised directly with me, and anyway I did not think it was helpful for me to become involved in this way. When I communicated this to the officer I had to endure the feeling that my refusal would result in Mary not being housed. On another occasion a psychiatric social worker telephoned to ask whether I would discuss my work with Mary. She wanted to know what sort of areas I was dealing with, as it had been decided that Mary and her children should be seen for family therapy and the workers did not want to cover the same ground. I said that I thought it was best if I did not talk about Mary, and again had to bear the anger caused by my unwillingness to discuss this client. Quite possibly both these workers were frustrated in their attempts to help Mary, her silence apparently resulting in a need to share information about her. At the time I felt, perhaps as Mary did, awkward, secretive and uncooperative.

The hardest call for me to manage was one from a therapist at a Family Centre. She had decided that Mary's panic attacks should be treated with behavioural techniques and said it was impossible to be certain about what Mary wanted for herself, as she 'refuses to answer questions'. The therapist went on to say that psychotherapy was notoriously bad at dealing with anxiety attacks but she did not want to do anything to undermine my work, which was why she needed information. 'Are you dealing with the panic?' she asked. I replied as I had done with the first two enquirers and again felt myself being experienced as obstructive. The therapist said that it was extremely unhelpful of me not to discuss my work. 'How can we know whether to refer her for this sort of treatment when you won't tell us whether you are dealing with anxiety issues?' I was then asked if I would agree to Mary seeing another therapist who would work in a 'more focused' way. I said that I appreciated there were doubts about what I was providing but I thought the decision about whether something else was started was best settled between Mary and the therapist.

Professionals working in different fields all have their own expertise and particular ways of working. It may be that these involve liaising with other workers, and of course there is nothing intrinsically wrong with this, but taking a different stance can put you in a lonely position, a position which may cause conflict with colleagues. If I put myself in the shoes of the housing officer, the social worker and the therapist, I can imagine how I must have appeared to them. They were doing what they thought was right and my stance was at odds with their beliefs. I know that many therapists would disagree with my approach, that sharing information about clients with professional colleagues is not deemed to be a breach of confidentiality. When a client is being seen by one therapist it is often considered professionally correct for another to check before any other sort of therapeutic intervention is offered. I don't think it is helpful for individuals to be seen by various different therapists, for splitting is then inevitable. What I mean by 'splitting' is that in the event of an individual deciding to see two therapists, there is the likelihood of one becoming the good object, the other the bad one. This will result in a situation whereby projections are never withdrawn, and thus the client avoids the reality of experiencing one person as the source of many different and often conflicting emotions. However, I think people have a right to discover this for themselves and it may be necessary for them to go through the experience before they can under-stand what they are doing. Of course, most therapists do not want to get drawn into the sort of confusion which results from clients involving many different workers in their difficulties, but should it be found that this is happening then it can be discussed with the client. This is rather different from making decisions for them, without consultation. I am not suggesting that these issues are unimportant, but simply that decisions should be taken by the therapist and the client together and not talked about with anyone other than the client.

I do not know what was going on between Mary and the family therapist but what seemed to be happening was that anxiety was not being contained. I could only go on what I knew: Mary kept on coming to see me and although she hardly spoke at all in these meetings, she seemed to find the experience of being with me helpful. On one of the few occasions on which she did speak, she told me that she used her time with me to think about her life, her childhood, her mother, her absent father and her own children. Mary may have been silent but she was finding her own way of using the therapy.

It took me several months to learn how to be with her in the way she needed me to be. At first, as everyone else seemed to do, I tried to encourage her to talk but gradually I came to understand that she experienced comments or interventions as intrusive. Like the other workers I felt concerned about Mary's life outside the consulting room in what was clearly a harsh and difficult world, but slowly I became more confident in her ability to manage these realities. I cannot know with any certainty that our work together was beneficial – I only occasionally heard of small improvements in Mary's life. More often I was told how difficult things were. What I did know was that Mary's relationship with me was important, as she kept on coming despite all the external difficulties. The panic attacks were seldom mentioned although once, at the time of the call about behavioural therapy, Mary said that she did not experience these feelings in her sessions with me. She did not elaborate but it could be that my acceptance of Mary's need not to speak, coupled with an ability to withstand the demands made on me and the pressure to speak about her, helped Mary to internalize me as a therapist who believed in her ability to manage life herself. At times it felt very lonely, particularly when my belief in myself as a therapist, and in Mary as an adult able to live an independent life of her own was called into question.

Communications from colleagues regarding clients should not be brushed aside as unwelcome intrusions. The anxiety that has been provoked should be acknowledged and understood. The tightrope we walk is how to listen to these concerns with sympathy, whilst resisting the temptation to talk about the content of the therapy.

THIRD-PARTY ANXIETIES

Before I discuss the next case it seems appropriate to make some generalizations about the anxieties that are stirred up in those who refer individuals, or who have close contact with someone in therapy, and how these anxieties can lead to a need for contact with the therapist. One of the ways of thinking about these contacts is in terms of parental anxieties. All therapists will know about these sorts of feelings, as they are part of the work. After particularly difficult sessions we may be beset with doubts: will our clients be all right, will they manage on their own, was what we said helpful, should we have said something different? In the session clients look to us for help, but when they leave we have to let them go to manage on their own. We must all be familiar with clients who leave their despair with us; we feel anxious and concerned, only to find when they return that life has been going well for them. It is not that our anxiety has been pointless or misplaced, but rather we may well be doing what all parents do for their children; containing the anxiety, holding on to the fear that the child will not manage for itself.

One of the hardest aspects of learning to let children go is for parents to accept that parts of their children's lives are private. Perhaps it is these feelings which come into focus for parents, husbands, wives, partners, relatives and friends, as well as professional referrers, when someone they know and care about enters a relationship in which they have no part. This is paralleled in the therapeutic relationship: two people meet together regularly and if the client will not reveal what is going on to an anxious outside party, then the feeling of exclusion may be dealt with by appealing to the therapist. Clients can talk about their therapy to third parties as much as they want to, for this is their right. Therapists are in a different position: either they have promised confidentiality or, although it may not be put into words, they have an internal belief in the importance of privacy. If we are going to maintain the frame, the container for the process of therapy, we can see that all anxieties should be brought back into the primary relationship, that of therapist and client. If we also see this primary relationship as standing for all the relationships the client has with people in the world outside, we can begin to see how fruitless it will be for the therapist to try to diminish anxiety by entering into discussions with third parties. In other situations it may be quite appropriate for contact to be made with another worker. A housing officer may require proof of homelessness: details of the individual's current situation, a letter from a GP which draws attention to the patient's state of health. This is factual information which may be needed before a decision can be taken regarding the allocation of scarce resources. The therapeutic task is to understand the client. However, therapists are not dealing in facts alone. We may be told of appalling experiences, hardships and tribulations that are quite overwhelming, and these may be true factually as well as emotionally, but this is not the point. We are not concerned with judging the objective truth of what our clients tell us but in understanding what their experiences of life have meant to them. For me to have written a report on Mary so that she could be housed was not appropriate. Of course I would have liked her to move out of the hostel, as I could imagine how difficult it must have been to try to bring up two young children there. However, I was not in a position to know that Mary was more deserving than anyone else who was homeless, and to write a report on her would have made me into a social worker or housing officer rather than a therapist. It is important to bear in mind that wherever possible the therapist is concerned with understanding rather than action. Social service workers have to make decisions based on factual information so that the fairest outcome is reached. They have to act. For the therapist to stray into this realm is to confuse roles, and although writing reports about people or taking actions for them may help in the short term, it will frustrate the longer-term goal of autonomy.

JOHN: PARENTAL INTRUSION

I now want to return to my work with John, first described in Chapter 4. Let me reiterate how in the initial consultation my own internal beliefs broke down under pressure. Despite the fact that I believed the most helpful thing was for John and I to meet without anyone else in attendance, I agreed to his mother being present at the beginning of the interview. After the initial consultation I saw him for six more sessions before I again became involved with his parents. In these six meetings John was becoming engaged in the process of therapy, mainly by my leaving him to determine what we talked about. By entering into a dialogue regarding the pattern on a carpet in my consulting room, which he kept staring at, I was allowed to know more about John and his concerns. He commented on the different flowers all apparently growing out of one central stem. This led on to a Matisse print on the wall, the shapes in which reminded him of butterflies. Did I know that they ate butterflies in some countries? An interesting aunt of his had supplied this information. He spoke about having his own garden and how he liked to grow flowers, herbs and shrubs. He did not like using pesticides, preferring more natural forms of control. I heard about his dog Sandy and how John felt uncertain about her attending obedience classes. 'After all she is a living creature, she may not want to.' He had sympathies with the Animal Liberationists although he was doubtful about their methods. At first I added a few questions and comments but as the session progressed the communication would become entirely John's. I listened, only once making a direct connection between his doubts regarding obedience classes and his own predicament: 'A bit like you and school.' John smiled.

It is possible to see a little of what might have been troubling John. He puzzled over the carpet and thought it unlikely that such different flowers could really grow from one plant. This reference to differences might have been connected with conflicts over fusion and separation. Was it possible to be part of a family and yet be separate, different from the other members? This theme of difference carries on into the thought about customs in other countries, eating butterflies not being the norm in England. Should his dog Sandy be forced to conform or should she be allowed to remain herself, disobedient? John admired those who believed in the rights of all living creatures but was worried about their methods, perhaps a reference to his own violent feelings. I did not put these thoughts into words, apart from the one comment I made about school, as it still felt very early days. John was discovering that he could set the pace and determine what was talked about.

At the end of the sixth of our regular meetings John left and I heard the car door slam and the engine start. A minute or two later the bell rang. I opened the door to find John standing on the step, his mother a little behind. He looked very upset and anxious. John muttered something that was incomprehensible apart from the word Friday. I asked him to repeat what he had said and Mrs Wright put her hand on her son's back. Hesitatingly, John told me that he wanted to come to see me on Fridays as well as Tuesdays. I suggested we talk about this together when he came for his next session the following week. Mrs Wright seemed to push John forward slightly. 'Can I come this Friday?' he asked. I said this would not be possible but we could talk about it again on Tuesday.

This time I felt I had contained the anxiety, in so far as I had not allowed myself to be rushed into action before I understood what the request meant, and whether it was what John wanted himself. But I was concerned by Mrs Wright's apparent need to push John into asking for something that may have been what she desired rather than what he wanted. I wondered what would happen next and how best to address the question of two sessions with John.

On Monday morning, five minutes before I was due to start work, Mrs Wright telephoned. She told me that they (presumably she and her husband) had decided to put John's treatment with me into abeyance. Her son, she said, was terribly anxious to get back to school and last Friday they had gone to see a psychiatrist. He had diagnosed John as suffering from post-traumatic shock syndrome and it was decided that he should enter hospital for intensive treatment. I felt shocked and upset. Trying to think quickly I went through the options. John's parents had a right to decide what treatment their son received. If I was antagonistic I might sabotage any possibility of further work with him. Nevertheless, I also had a duty to John; our relationship was important and I did not want him to feel that I did not recognize this. I decided to accept defeat gracefully but to tell Mrs Wright that as I would not be seeing John again, I would write to him. I also said that I was sorry about her decision. Mrs Wright intervened to say that John's contact with me was only in abeyance, and would it be acceptable if they contacted me again in the future. I agreed and said I would be pleased to hear from her. Mrs Wright appeared to soften, 'It is a pity, John was starting to relate to you.' There was no time for further discussion so I brought our conversation to a close.

I felt upset, angry and frustrated and it was only later in supervision that I was able to explore my own feelings further. I felt that my authority had been undermined and in the face of an arbitrary decision I had quickly let my own sense of knowing what was best slip away. This involved personal difficulties, and was not explicable purely in terms of Mrs Wright's action. I decided to write to John and to his parents suggesting that he and I have a last meeting so that we could bring our work together to a close. I deliberately made my letter to both parents and a separate letter was sent to John. The reason for addressing Mr Wright as well as Mrs Wright stemmed from the thought that, as well as separation anxiety concerning mother and son, oedipal feelings involving the triangular relationship between John and his parents might also be of significance.

You will probably know that in the Greek myth Oedipus is abandoned because of a prophecy, which he then unwittingly fulfils by murdering his father and marrying his mother. This story is taken to be an expression of a universal experience, one that involves conflicting feelings of love and rivalry. We might think that when he was abandoned and left to die on the mountainside, Oedipus would have experienced very terrible emotions. These could be seen to stand for the feelings children experience when excluded from the intimacy of the parental relationship, an intimacy which they can neither understand nor share. The fact that Oedipus did not know what he was doing can be seen as an expression of his unconscious desires. Children sometimes find it difficult to distinguish their feelings from their actions – an angry thought can feel like a dreadful deed. Thus the Oedipus myth can be read on two levels: a literal account of patricide and incest, or as an expression of a universal predicament experienced in childhood.

The 'oedipal feelings' I thought might be significant in John's case, refer to unconscious anxieties he might have regarding his relationship with his mother. I had been aware that John's father seemed to be taking little part in decisions regarding his son's treatment. This was why I decided to write to husband and wife rather than just to the mother. I also thought that by addressing the parents in a joint letter and sending a separate one to John, I would be underlining his separateness. Interestingly, it was Mr Wright who contacted me on receipt of my letter and the meeting was agreed. He went into some detail about the new treatment, which was clearly behavioural therapy, and added that John was full of anxiety and begging for something to get him back to school. It was his son's pleading, he said, that had made them decide to try this new approach. I made no comment on their decision, except to acknowledge how desperate they felt about getting results. Mr Wright emphasized that John's contact with me was not curtailed but suspended, and asked whether they could be in touch again. I agreed.

In working with a child the frame poses special problems, particularly in private practice when the initial negotiations have to be made
between parent and therapist. In a public setting it is possible for
'children' to make their own arrangements. Here I am talking not about
very small children but young people aged 13 or more. When they are
younger than this they are usually seen with parents in Child and Family
Clinics. In a young people's agency parents can make the initial 'phone
call to find out about the organization but they can then be encouraged
to let the young people make their own appointments. When parents
bring the child to a clinic or a centre there is usually somewhere for them
to wait until the consultation is concluded. Of course this doesn't mean
that parents won't ask to see the therapist, and all the difficulties of
protecting the therapy are still encountered. What is different is that
often the agency will be in the locality, and is easily accessible. It is also
accessible in economic terms: subsidies enable those on low incomes to
be seen at reduced rates, and those with no income, either through
unemployment or because they are too young to work, can be seen
without charge.

This is not true of private practice: children rely on parents to take
them to the therapist and to pay the fee. Moreover, they have to accept
a parental decision as to whether the therapy should continue or not.
Children do not have the right to decide for themselves what they want
and it is not possible for the therapy to be contained in the way it would
be with an adult. Nevertheless, the therapist can ensure the child's right
to privacy. It was a great temptation to reveal the content of my sessions
with John in an effort to demonstrate that we might be getting somewhere, however slowly. I might have told Mr and Mrs Wright that, in
my opinion, it was not helpful for them to break off the treatment to start
another, particularly when we were only just beginning. I could have
asked to speak to the psychiatrist to discuss John's difficulties so that we
could reach an understanding of what was best for him. I don't feel any
absolute conviction that what I did was right, and indeed I was beset
with doubts. However, if my original hypothesis regarding John and his
mother and the anxiety about separation was correct, then I doubt
whether getting into a battle over who could help him the most would
really have improved matters. My distress at John's brutal separation
from me was contained, perhaps at first it was too contained, I was in
danger of letting him go entirely. By asking firmly for a last session and
indicating that I believed this to be the right way of working, I re-
established authority with John's parents. This was necessary before I
could understand what their decision might mean to him. In this

instance, John, his needs and his feelings, almost got lost amongst the adults who were fighting to help him.

Despite firm convictions regarding the importance of a confidential relationship, my own beliefs are not unshakeable. I still get moments of uncertainty, particularly when I feel frightened. Sometimes this is because clients want me to talk about them to a doctor or a social worker, or when I feel concern about an individual who has suicidal thoughts. At other times I feel pressure from colleagues or from referrers who want to know about the therapy. What I do know is that any breach, whether instigated by the client, by the therapist, or a third party, will have consequences. Absolute rules of conduct are not desirable, as they result in therapists who place theory above the individual needs of their clients. All we can do is to treat each case on its merits, do our best, and be open to the possibility of mistakes. Luckily for us, most people are forgiving and allow us to learn from our errors.

Chapter 7

Ongoing work

When the framework has been established and the offer of regular appointments accepted there then follows a period of settling into the therapeutic work. With some clients a sense of engagement occurs quickly, others take longer, and there are also those with whom uncertainty is ever present. Whilst these different feelings can be understood in terms of transference and countertransference, it is also important to examine therapist interventions as a way of monitoring their impact on the client. It is all too easy to forget how our words may be experienced and before we speak it is useful to use Casement's concept of trial identification (Casement 1990). By putting ourselves in the place of the client and imagining how our interpretation might be heard, we can be sensitive in our choice of words. At times we all re-interpret or misinterpret what is said to us, but if the therapist's words spring from preconceived notions unrelated to the individuals they are meant to address then they will have little emotional meaning. We can never know with absolute certainty that the client is engaged, and however solid the therapeutic alliance may seem we can never be entirely sure that the client will return for the next session. By keeping this possibility in mind, complacency can be avoided. When a client drops out without explanation, or when the therapist is abruptly told of a decision to stop coming, we need to think about how we may have contributed to this decision.

In this chapter I am going to describe aspects of ongoing work with clients, two of whom, Wendy and John, I have already introduced, the third, whom I will call Margaret, being an example of someone who left after eight sessions. One of the reasons for this termination occurred because I had not understood anxieties that had in fact been voiced in the initial consultation. An assumption on my part of what I considered to be the best way of managing the arrangements for ongoing work was another factor. The failure to connect the client's fears with the way in which the offer of regular sessions was heard resulted in the therapy breaking down. I will start with Margaret because I think this case underlines the dangers of therapist complacency and how this can foster a false sense of engagement. A premature ending is almost inevitable if clients are left with the feeling that their most basic concerns are not being addressed.

MARGARET: A FAILURE OF UNDERSTANDING

Margaret came for help because of uncontrollable grief over the decision of her fourteen-year-old son to leave home to take up residence with his father, Margaret's ex-husband. I saw how this grief was experienced when Margaret cried desperately, the tears coming in short bursts which were then rigidly controlled as she seemed, literally, to pull herself together. She talked almost non-stop and I heard that although it had originally been her doctor's suggestion to see a therapist, it was in fact her present partner's statement that her thoughts were 'mad' which had actually made Margaret do so. The madness referred to aggressive impulses towards her ex-husband's new wife, who seemed to Margaret to be 'stealing' her son. I think it was my holding of this terror of madness which began to engage her. I gave no reassurance but simply allowed Margaret to cry. As her distress lessened she said, 'I don't think Tom thinks I'm mad. What he said was really a joke, but I feel as if I'm going mad.' I said it sounded very frightening and Margaret cried again. When she stopped she launched into detailed descriptions of various incidents that had occurred in the family. I got caught up in the immediacy of these events and allowed the anxiety about madness to get lost.

It was hard to make space to discuss arrangements for regular meetings but when I finally managed to do so there were only about ten minutes to go before the end of the consultation. Margaret immediately accepted my offer of regular meetings and asked only one question, 'How long will it take?' I made a rather generalized comment about this anxiety rather than trying to understand what it meant to Margaret as an individual. She responded by saying, 'You think it better if I just keep on coming until things are sorted out?' We were nearing the end of the interview and I was becoming concerned with bringing it to a close. Instead of really thinking about how my words had been experienced, I said something like this: 'You have told me of a lot of feelings which have been bottled up over the years and I think it would be helpful for you to have an opportunity to talk about them.' My answer to her question was not really an answer at all, but another rather general statement, nor did what I say address the anxiety underlying her question. Instead, the suggestion that she should have time to talk about her difficulties, an unspecified time, was experienced by Margaret, I learnt later, as a life-sentence. She had told me about the unbearable feelings experienced when her son had decided to leave home, how this had stirred up in her aggressive thoughts so overwhelmingly that she thought she was going mad. I had now set up a situation in which she felt I was going to hang on to her forever, just as she wanted to hang on to her son. Margaret felt that she had no control over how long the relationship with me was to last. I had heard about dependence and independence, the frightening feelings that resulted from separation, the longing to remain fused, the fear of never being separate, yet none of these had been addressed in terms of Margaret's relationship with me.

If the client is having difficulties over separation then it is essential that the therapist is experienced as someone who understands and is able to manage these feelings. In retrospect, I don't think I should necessarily have changed my offer of an open-ended relationship with Margaret but what I should have done was to understand what this meant to her and put my understanding into words.

In the ensuing weeks Margaret continued to talk non-stop. I made few comments, thinking that she was experiencing relief in having somewhere to pour out all her feelings. I even congratulated myself on not having got drawn into a statement about the length of our work together. I had made an assumption that this would be unhelpful, an assumption based on theoretical knowledge, not on Margaret's predicament and how this might relate to her relationship with me. The situations she described were complex and as more and more difficulties were revealed I was convinced our contact would be long-term. At the beginning of sessions Margaret would ask herself a question, 'How am I?' as if I had asked it. She would then tell me what had been happening in the previous week. There were small signs of improvement, she had done what I had said and it had been helpful. Again I felt self-congratulatory as I knew I had not made the suggestions Margaret apparently heard me making, and it seemed as if she was conducting her own therapy. I provided the containment that was enabling her to find her own answers – an ideal situation. What I was not doing was processing Margaret's outpourings. If I had been I would either have found words that were containing or my silence would have been an active one. What I mean is this: when the therapist follows the unconscious meaning of what is being communicated, this understanding is experienced by the client at an unconscious level and there is an emotional rapport, so that explicit statements of understanding are unnecessary. I was too engaged in listening to the surface or manifest content of Margaret's communication and although I avoided making suggestions or giving advice, Margaret must have felt she was speaking into a void. I was biding my time, waiting until I felt I had something useful to say. Margaret's readiness to talk made me think we had all the time in the world. My own exhaustion at the end of sessions should have alerted me to what Margaret was feeling.

At the beginning of the eighth and what was to be our final meeting Margaret appeared awkward. Almost before she sat down she started speaking. 'I should tell you I won't be coming any more after today.' I felt shocked, perhaps as Margaret had when her son announced his decision. At first she told me that leaving the therapy was because 'things' were so much better, she did not feel so desperate about her son, and she had got 'on top of things'. She and Tom, her second husband, had been able to talk about his feelings of having to care for a ready-made family, and of Margaret's fears that he did not love the children of her first marriage as he did their own child. These were positive developments but I was also told of a new and extremely upsetting situation. Clearly there were many 'things' that were far from better and this rather vague term which kept on recurring may have been a reference to the still unspeakable anxieties which had not been addressed in her relationship with me.

Gradually it emerged that my failure to understand how terrifying it had been to Margaret not to have any limit set to the therapy, was what lay behind her decision to stop coming. The previous week she had been telling a friend about her problems and had suddenly thought how she looked forward to talking to me. 'I realized,' Margaret said, 'that I was becoming dependent on you.' This had been an alarming idea. Margaret then told me that she had wanted me to suggest meeting, 'for four weeks, or six weeks or something like that. I wouldn't have minded if I then saw you for six more weeks, but when you didn't suggest any limit I thought it would just go on and on. I thought I'd be seeing you forever. There are so many things I could tell you about. Different things keep on coming up. I could tell you about my mother but I don't want to get into that.'

In the transference I had become the mother who could not let go: Margaret had experienced my lack of understanding over the length of contact as evidence that I wanted her to keep on coming forever. The arrangements I made had played into her fear of dependency; she also felt concerned that her decision to stop the meetings would be seen by me as wrong and that I would urge her to stay. I had to acknowledge, to myself, that this was indeed what I wanted to do but clearly it was not what was required. In the session I tried to find words that would address the situation yet still leave Margaret free to stay or go, a decision that could be based on something other than flight into health – having to move away from the situation causing conflict by convincing herself and me that her problems were solved. I could not find the right interpretation and therefore it seemed to me that the most helpful behaviour to model was acceptance. At the end of our time Margaret asked whether she could contact me again, 'if things get difficult'.

Later, I realized that I had been put in a double-bind and had I been able to articulate the position I was in I might have enabled Margaret to stay. The interpretation could have been: 'Your decision to stop seeing me has come about through your fear that you will become dependent. If I urge you to stay you will feel that this is what I want and that I will never let you go. If I agree to your going you may feel that I am not willing to keep on trying to understand how frightening dependency is to you.'

In trying to evaluate the eight sessions I had to acknowledge that although there had been an improvement in communication between Margaret and her husband, little else had been achieved. I suspect her reassurance to me – 'things are a lot better' – was a manifest statement and that the new situation which was so distressing, evidenced a more accurate state of how matters really stood. We have to live with our mistakes, together with the knowledge that failures can result in clients not wishing to give therapy another chance, despite their kindness in reassuring the therapist of how much they have been helped.

WENDY: ANXIETY CONTAINED

The anxieties I had not understood with Margaret were also a feature of my contact with Wendy, who was discussed in Chapter 4, but in this case I was better able to contain and understand them. In the initial consultation I had told Wendy that she might have to wait several months before I could see her on a regular basis but in fact only seven weeks elapsed before I was able to write offering these meetings.

For the first few months of our contact I was quite overwhelmed by the situations she related and the anxiety they caused. I would hear of family rows and how, after them, Wendy would go over and over what had been said. She became convinced that in her work as a cleaner she had stolen money from her employer. She had looked at a pile of coins kept in a bowl and thought she could take them, and that no one would know. Wendy then became convinced she had taken them. Her meetings with the psychiatrist were minutely examined, the words he had spoken taken apart, repeated to me, interpreted, then re-interpreted and taken as evidence that she should do this, or then again that. Incidents from her past were talked about over and over again. Wendy was convinced that she had sexually abused a child entrusted to her care. She knew she had not but still the thought that she might have came back to torment her.

Her distress was so great that initially I fell into the trap I had avoided in our first meeting – of trying to reassure Wendy. I did this by attempting to interpret her fears through an intellectual understanding of what might lie behind them, and by drawing attention to how thoughts seemed to become synonymous with actions. All these interpretations did was to confuse Wendy more. What did I mean? Would I explain myself? Did I mean this? Did I mean that? Any attempt to connect events from the past with those in the present led to more questions. Did I really think the past had anything to do with her present difficulties? Didn't I think, as her mother and her psychiatrist thought, that she should put the past behind her? I was all at sea but very gradually I learnt to simply be with Wendy and to allow myself to feel as confused as she did. Something I was aware of, and which slowly helped me to contain these feelings of confusion, was the frame. No matter how often Wendy told me that she did not see how counselling could help, or that she felt no better, or how she longed to get a job which involved contact with other young people but couldn't, no matter how often we went over the same incidents, she kept on coming to see me. She was always on time, always came with her money ready to give me on the day the bill was due, and at the end of sessions Wendy would invariably ply me with questions which I managed not to answer. Gradually I began to realize that what was most important was to be with Wendy, to maintain the framework for care and to contain anxiety.

Now the location for our meetings involved clients in having to report to a receptionist, who then telephoned the therapist to announce their arrival. There was no real reason for this to happen after the initial consultation, other than convenience for the therapist, and one day Wendy told me how much she hated this arrangement. She felt the receptionist could see into her mind and waiting downstairs left her feeling confused and upset. I thought about this and said, 'You are telling me how unhelpful it is to have other people involved in what you thought was a private relationship.' This was the first comment I made which really seemed to reach Wendy, as she went on to talk about her fears that I and the psychiatrist were in communication and that we probably laughed together about her. She said again how awkward she felt having to sit downstairs and asked if she could come straight up to see me without checking in at the reception desk. I thought about her request and said, 'You are telling me again that our relationship should be private and that you don't want anyone else to be involved. Yes, I think in future it would be more helpful if you came straight up.'

This is what happened and I used this understanding to change the arrangements, not just for Wendy but also for other clients. I discovered a vacant room on the same floor as mine and told clients that if they were early they could wait there until it was time for them to see me. In fact Wendy never waited in this room as she always arrived precisely on time, and it must have seemed inexplicable that prior to this change she had to wait until the receptionist announced her arrival. Since at times there were others waiting in this communal area, for all sorts of different appointments unconnected with therapy, Wendy's feeling that her relationship with me was not being kept private was quite correct. This incident gave me guidance when on another occasion Wendy said she wanted me to speak to her psychiatrist about the anti-depressants she was taking. She felt uncertain as to whether they were helping her or not and said that her psychiatrist had suggested Wendy ask me whether I would telephone him to discuss what I thought. The manifest content of Wendy's communication was to agree with the psychiatrist and when I said I did not think it would be helpful for me to make decisions for her, she was at first upset and angry. I said that she had already told me how important it was for our relationship not to involve other people and how upsetting it felt to think she was being talked about. And although I appreciated that it was difficult for her that I was not agreeing to her request, I thought it would be best if I did not discuss her with anyone else.

When therapists use their judgement in sticking to one of the rules of the frame, because it is felt to be right in the particular instance, it would be nice to have immediate confirmation that this has been experienced as helpful. This did not happen and although I think my decision not to talk about Wendy was right, this only became a certainty after repeated testing out and a gradual lessening of anxiety. At the time I had to bear her feeling that I was being unhelpful. There were many other occasions when she would ask me for advice or guidance and it was difficult not to give in to these pressures but I kept in mind all the incidents she had told me of when all this did was to confuse her further.

After several months Wendy decided to go on a training scheme which involved attending classes in secretarial skills prior to a work placement. The young man who sat next to her in class lent her some paper and Wendy became convinced she had stolen it. Anything said to her, either by fellow students or the teacher, was dissected for hidden meanings when she was alone at night, convincing her that she was mad. She would still ask me whether I thought she was crazy but seemed less anxious when I said nothing. I did not attempt to interpret these thoughts because I had already discovered that this plunged Wendy into just the situation that was so painful to her. Anything I said seemed to be experienced as an intrusion of my thoughts into her head, resulting in extreme anxiety as she tried to disentangle them from her own thoughts. Although Wendy was still talking about the miseries she experienced in her relationships outside the sessions, her contact with me appeared less anxiety-ridden. My growing ability to keep myself separate from her began to enable Wendy to experience herself as separate from me. I was aware that her decision to take the first steps towards getting a job was important, as this was what she had told me was so vital in our first meeting.

One day, after we had been meeting for nine months, Wendy arrived in an extremely agitated state and told me that in four weeks' time she was to start her placement. It was in the workplace of her choice, which she was pleased about, but would mean she could no longer attend her meetings with me. What did I think? Should she go on the placement or should she continue her counselling? Was counselling really helpful? What did I think? Would it be possible for her to come at another time? I said nothing, first because I knew this was a decision Wendy had to make for herself and second, because I now knew from experience that whatever I said would cause further confusion. Wendy continued to bombard me with thoughts and questions. 'I do sometimes think it's helpful but I'm not sure. What do you think? I remember you couldn't see me in the evenings when I first came so I don't suppose you can now. I do want to get a job but I don't know if I'm ready to. What if I stop coming to see you and I get worse? Will you see me again if I stop coming?' Slowly the questions abated and Wendy became more reflective, there were pauses between her thoughts, and she now seemed to be having a conversation with herself. 'I really do want a job. I do want to get out of the house and meet people. I expect I'll find it difficult at first. I suppose I'll worry about what other people are thinking. I always do.'

This dialogue with herself went on for some time and then Wendy said, 'I think I do want to go on the placement. But I do want to keep on seeing you. Would that be possible?' I explained that I did not have an immediate vacancy in the evenings but if she wanted me to I could let her know as soon as a time became available. Wendy said that this was what she wanted, although in this session and in the ones leading up to her last before the placement, anxiety about whether it was the right decision was still apparent.

I knew that Wendy still had many difficulties but for me to have tried to influence her decision about whether to continue her therapy or go on the placement, would have been to undermine her right to determine things for herself. Two months passed before I was able to write offering a time for an evening meeting and when she arrived Wendy started talking straight away. She had wondered whether I had forgotten her. She was learning how to type and the other people in the office where she worked sometimes laughed at how anxious she was. She had gone to a disco with her sister and a young man had shown some interest in her. She had felt quite pleased but didn't want to go out with him. She felt too frightened to start this sort of relationship, and anyway she wondered whether he really liked her or whether she had misunderstood his interest. Perhaps some of these concerns were about me and my interest in her and what it might mean, but by now I knew that it was better to leave Wendy free to make her own connections.

We went on meeting at the new time for another three months before Wendy was offered a permanent job, making the early evening hour of her appointment impossible to keep. During this period she gradually began to tell me about her father and the terrible distress she had experienced when he died. It became clear that although Wendy's problems were exacerbated by the tragic circumstances of her father's death, the difficulties went back to her earliest years. She found great relief in the fact that I did not interpret these problems solely in terms of her relationship with her father and his suicide which, perhaps under-standably, was how her mother and the rest of the family understood the difficulty. When Wendy told me about the job she had been offered there was no doubt in her mind that she wanted to accept it, but she also wanted to keep on seeing me. This time her concerns were centred around how I must feel. She knew that she would have to wait again and was willing to do so but wondered how I felt about this. Did I mind? Would it be possible to find another time? Would I be hurt that she was putting the job before me? I simply said that it would be possible to resume our meetings and that as soon as a later time became available it would be offered to her.

On occasions when the frame was weak (when she had to report to a receptionist), or when it was altered (when she could no longer come at the agreed time), Wendy's anxiety became intense. In the first instance the anxiety was provoked by my error in not ensuring our relationship was a private one, in the second it was because of Wendy's decision to take up the offer of work. By leaving her free, either to take the job or to continue seeing me at the arranged time, I was letting her determine her own actions. The consequence of this was that Wendy had to manage her anxious feelings during the waiting period. The fact that I had been able to contain her fears (manifested in the constant questions) and my own feelings (concern about Wendy) enabled her to decide what she wanted, and also to wait with increasing certainty for the resumption of our relationship.

JOHN: A SAD ENDING, AND THEN AN ANGRY ENDING

Like Wendy my contact with John was also subject to interruption. You will remember that I left him in Chapter 6 with our work terminated but had written to him and to his parents suggesting we had a final meeting in which we could take our leave of each other. This was agreed and in this last meeting John was uncommunicative, silent and seemed despairing. I said little, other than to acknowledge the fact that this was our last meeting and to wonder how it felt to him to have no control over what happened. At the end he said goodbye politely and left.

About ten days later I had a telephone call from Mr Wright to say that John had refused to go into the clinic for the treatment that had been arranged for him and was being 'extremely un-cooperative'. Apparently he had told his parents that he wanted to go on seeing me and Mr Wright was telephoning to ask whether I would be willing to resume the meetings. I agreed to do so and the arrangements were made. It would be satisfying to go on to describe how I was able to understand John's difficulties and help him to start living a more fulfilling life, but reality is rarely like that.

What actually happened was that John returned for five more sessions and then stopped coming because he no longer wanted to. I cannot be sure why this was but I think it was due to my leaving him in silence for too long. I was so aware of the need not to intrude and not to seem to be determining what he talked about that I allowed John's anxiety to become overwhelming. In our last meeting he became extremely angry and aggressive telling me that I should ask him questions, that I was the expert and therefore should know what to do to help him. I attempted to understand these demands in terms of what had happened to him in the past, when other people had made decisions for him, and how he might have experienced this, that it had perhaps made him angry and yet now I was not telling him what he should do he felt confused and angry with me. But this did not seem to help, for the following week I received a call to say that John refused to come to his appointment. I asked if I could speak to him but he would not come to the telephone, so I told his mother I would be keeping the time open the following week and would write to John to let him know that I would be available. He did not come and when his father rang to say that John was adamant about not seeing me any more, I suggested we respect his son's decision. I wrote to John saying that I hoped he would get in touch with me again if ever he wanted to.

Before I received further news I thought about John a great deal and tried to understand what might have been happening in our contact. In our first meeting, which had been so chaotic, John had told me of an incident that had occurred at his school. One afternoon in a break between lessons John had got into an argument with his peers, one of whom had accused him of being 'rude'. Later on when John was sitting in the classroom this boy had suddenly come over, stamped on his foot and broken one of his toes. The injury resulted in John going to hospital, where his foot was strapped, and from then on he refused to go to school. John himself made no connection between this incident and his fear of going out. Indeed he made it quite clear that he did not want to discuss what had happened since it was, in his words, 'completely irrelevant'. However, he related these events to me with such anxiety that I realized that although John could not connect the attack made on him with his refusal to leave home, there was something very important underlying this incident.

One way of understanding what happened would be to see this as a young boy's natural fear of aggressive feelings in his fellow pupils. Another way might be to see it in terms of castration anxiety related to the re-emergence of oedipal feelings in adolescence. John had been very specific when he told me that the boy had accused him of being rude, an accusation which he felt was unjustified. Now to be rude is to be aggressive but it is also a word often used by children to refer to anything connected with genitals, and the ultimate expression of adult sexuality is through genital union. John was adolescent and in this stage of development young people are concerned with establishing an identity separate from their parents; one that will eventually enable them to form sexual relationships with the partner of their choice. John had passed through the latency period (from about five until the onset of puberty sexual evolution takes a pause) and now oedipal feelings would be re-emerging, to be worked through so that he could become adult. The oedipal stage involves the male child having tender feelings towards the mother and aggressive feelings towards the father, his rival for his mother's love. These feelings are very frightening, for his rival is also someone he loves and admires, the result being ambivalence, an admixture of love and hate. These feelings are projected on to the father who is then seen as having aggressive feelings towards the child, the result of which will be castration. This doesn't mean castration in the literal sense, although this may have been a reality in our dim and distant past, but more a sense that the child will be punished severely for his desires, that something of value will be taken from him.

When John told me about the boy breaking his toe I knew that I was being told something of great importance. I tried to help him to tell me more but only two other facts emerged: the boy who caused the injury had been punished, and the headteacher had assured John that there would be no recurrence of the aggression. Clearly this had done nothing to alleviate his anxiety. If we think about what he told me, it was in fact John who seemed to have had aggressive or rude feelings first, and it was because of these feelings that the other boy had broken his toe. If we imagine that John was trying to manage his own aggressive feelings towards his father, and that they had been replaced by aggressive feelings towards other males, his peers at school, then we might say that his classmate's retaliation was experienced by John as standing for castration by the father. His worst fears had been realized and now the anxiety he felt regarding first his father then his peers, had been replaced by a more general anxiety in connection with school.

I thought particularly hard about two factors in our contact. First, the fact that John had been able to reject his parents' view of what was best for him, the behavioural treatment, thus establishing himself as a person who could make his own decisions. And second, I wondered whether the fact that John had been able to be angry with me might have been experienced as helpful to him. I could be seen as an authority figure standing for his father, and in our last meeting he had been openly angry and hostile towards me. The fact that I did not retaliate by meeting aggression with aggression might result in a modification of John's anxieties. I had also respected his right to decide not to see me but had let him know, through the letter inviting him to be in touch again should he want to, that there were no hard feelings.

Some two weeks later John's father rang to say he wanted me to know that his son was starting to go out more. Previously he had been unable to leave the house alone and usually either his mother or his father accompanied John wherever he went. Early one evening John had got his bike out of the garage and casually told his father that he was going for a ride. Mr Wright said he felt something had changed, however slightly, and that he had wanted me to know. I thought this was a generous gesture on his part, and although I felt disappointment at the short and rather chaotic contact, it seemed possible that John's anger with me – his own decision to end our relationship and my acceptance of this – may have helped him to take the first steps towards independence. This is of course a positive view and one based more on what I was told by his father than on anything John said, but the very fact that there seemed to be more interaction between father and son, I thought to be a change which might augur well for John's future development.

As I pointed out earlier, working with a child makes it impossible to maintain the frame in quite the way that is possible with an adult. Even so, an understanding of what this may mean, together with a respect for the privacy of the child, should inform the therapeutic work. In the ongoing process of therapy it is almost inevitable that the initial agreement will be broken or altered in some way and it is in remedying our errors, or understanding what alterations mean to individual clients, that therapists incorporate the concept of the frame into their work. Because her feelings were not understood, Margaret might be seen as experiencing the frame as a rigid structure from which she could never escape. The frame became a prison rather than a means for containing her fears. Wendy taught me how to provide a frame which was firm enough for her to experience the containment necessary for her to begin to move out into the world and make other relationships. In John's case, because of his age, it wasn't possible to provide a firm frame but at least he was able to have an experience in which he was allowed to make his own decisions.

Chapter 8

Money matters

Financial transactions are always tricky, particularly for therapists who are unfamiliar with this aspect of therapeutic work, and when faith in their own abilities is still somewhat shaky. Of course when we are inexperienced it is appropriate that the charge we make for our professional help is reflected in the fee. Undervaluing ourselves, however, can be as unhelpful as an over-evaluation of what we have to offer. These uncertainties can result in therapists avoiding discussion of the fee and what it may mean to clients to be asked to pay for therapy. Our own resistances can block exploration, which may result either in extreme rigidity or total flexibility. In the first case, this can result in a 'take it or leave it' attitude which allows no room for clients to express feelings about the fee; and in the second, going along with whatever clients suggest, thus leaving them with the feeling that therapists have no sense of their own worth. Therapists who feel confident that they have something of value to give will be more open to accepting any doubts that clients may have about them. If the therapist feels uneasy then this aspect of the frame will be avoided, and the client will sense the dis-ease which in turn will lead to difficulties later in the therapy.

There are many good arguments for psychological help being made more widely available to those who want it, and subsidized psychotherapy or counselling is one of the ways this can be achieved. But this in itself can cause problems, some of which were noted in Chapter 4, when I drew attention to the way in which 'bad' feelings can be projected out of the therapeutic relationship into the organization. We may believe very strongly in the idea of a society in which all citizens have equal access to mental health services, but therapists have to earn their livings, just like everyone else. This fact may be less obvious when the therapist receives payment from an institution rather than directly from a client, but it remains true.

If you are in private practice then the transaction will be made directly with the client and, as I suggested in Chapter 1, it is concerned with giving and receiving. Now it might be argued that the therapeutic encounter, in which a fee is charged by the therapist, is entirely different from the situation in the family where parents give their love unconditionally. However, although parents do not ask for financial rewards for their care, it is debatable as to whether love is always given freely. Each child in a unique family setting will learn that parents have needs as well as children, that certain behaviour elicits a positive response and other behaviour a negative one. In the best of families, whatever the child does, the parents respond lovingly, even when it is to curtail activities that are disapproved. In this way children come to know that they are loved, although some of the things they do, bad actions or destructive behaviour, are unacceptable. Unfortunately, few of us are always able to meet this ideal in terms of being parents and sometimes our children will feel that their badness results in a withdrawal of love. Thus we might say that whilst unconditional love is what we want as children and try to provide as parents, it is unlikely that this will always be achieved. It must also be acknowledged that the wish to reproduce ourselves involves complex motivations and certainly the feelings evoked in being a parent include, at times, feelings of hate as well as of love. On the face of it we might say that most people would prefer the therapist to see them for nothing, representing unconditional love, but if this should happen we might also think that the client who is not asked to pay will become puzzled and worried. How is it possible for therapists to maintain themselves? Do they have no needs? Do they live in the same sort of world as the client? The therapist who makes no charge might be seen as someone who has only love to give, a wonderful idea, but one that might leave clients very frightened of their own feelings of hate.

The fee, like other aspects of the frame, is concerned with two people. It represents a framework for a dual affiliation, client in relationship with therapist. If we accept that parents and children will experience all the complex emotions that are an essential part of human relationships, then we can see that this will involve love and hate, aggression and passivity, giving and taking, dependence and independence, and so on, ad infinitum. The fee, however it is accepted in the initial consultation, will often be experienced later as an imposition – a representation of the therapist's inability to love unconditionally. Of course the fee is an imposition, as therapists have to live and cannot give their time altruistically, although there may be times when we have to bear with a client who cannot or will not pay what is owing. It is important in these situations that the therapist understands what is going on and does not act in a retaliatory manner.

In this chapter I am going to give three examples of the way in which I handled difficulties that were manifested through the medium of money, and examine how these difficulties were connected with the client's pathology and with my own.

MATTHEW: A PROBLEM OF OVER-ACCOMMODATION

Matthew, as I will call him, was referred to me by a colleague who had offered this young man a consultation to help him find a therapist. When the referrer contacted me he said that Matthew was working but did not earn a great deal. The possibility of seeing a trainee therapist at a very reduced fee had been explored but the distance Matthew would have to travel to do this made it unacceptable. I said that I had a vacancy and would be willing to offer an initial consultation.

When I saw him Matthew was keen to take up the offer of regular appointments and said that in his meeting with my colleague it had been suggested he consider having two sessions per week. However, he felt he could not afford this and when I told him my fee Matthew thought that even once-weekly sessions would be difficult for him to manage. His wife, he said, was keen for him to continue his training, to improve his career prospects, and this necessitated him having one day a week off from his employment. She was less encouraging, Matthew said, when it came to spending money on therapy for himself. They were saving for a house and hoped to start a family in the not too distant future. After some discussion I agreed to see him at a reduced fee and went to considerable trouble to find a time that would fit in with the day he attended his course. Matthew did not drive so seeing me would involve a train journey and then a considerable walk to my consulting room. Now I was aware that in talking about his wife's doubts about the way he spent his money, Matthew was also talking about his own ambivalence regarding therapy. It was clearly something he wanted and yet each time he got close to making this a reality, difficulties were introduced which made it impossible. At the time, my decision to see him at a reduced fee was in part because I genuinely felt that money was tight. I also thought I was helping him overcome his resistance, which it could be argued was better left for Matthew to struggle with himself. Another factor was the referrer, a respected colleague of mine, who had already gone to considerable trouble to help Matthew find a therapist. I wanted to help him as well as Matthew and I suspect this desire to accommodate both referrer and client each played a part in my decision to reduce my fee.

During the first three months of our contact I had to work hard to understand how terribly difficult it was for Matthew to come at all. The train was either late or was cancelled, his colleagues at work talked about therapy being a waste of time, he did not know what I wanted him to say, he felt a failure in his work, in his studies, in his role as a husband and as a son, and now as a client with me. In listening to Matthew's reports of what his colleagues said, I knew that I was hearing about his own feelings, which for the moment could only be expressed through difficulties that were external rather than internal – how other people felt rather than how he felt. He constantly wondered whether he could or should continue to see me, and after six months of feeling that each session might be our last, I came to a better understanding of how tenuous relationships felt to Matthew, particularly if critical thoughts were openly expressed. I had also begun to understand that my agreeing to see him at a reduced fee might have been worrying to him. I heard of many occasions when by presenting himself as helpless and stupid he had been able to manipulate situations to what he thought were his own advantage. Matthew saw himself both as victim and aggressor, as both inferior and superior; what seemed impossible were relationships in which both parties felt equal and were honest with one another. In lowering the fee without clear evidence that he was unable to pay what I asked, I had fallen into the trap of seeing Matthew as a helpless victim of circumstance, a situation which he manipulated and which also allowed him to feel superior. Now although I had begun to understand my part in contributing to these difficulties, I had not as yet found an opportunity to make an interpretation to Matthew which made this apparent. The interpretations I tried out in my head, when I imagined how they might be experienced by Matthew, all sounded rather superior – words that might make him feel humiliated. So I decided to wait.

After about six months of attending regularly, despite all the external difficulties of unreliable trains, shortage of money and critical colleagues, Matthew gave me a cheque in payment of the bill I had given him the previous week. This was returned as there were insufficient funds in his bank account to meet it.

When he arrived for the next session I knew at once that Matthew had been notified of this, as even before he sat down he started to apologize. He was mortified and immediately handed me a cheque which he said was drawn on his wife's account. I said that I thought it would be better if I did not accept this and that it would be more helpful if he paid what he owed himself. Matthew told me that he never knew where he was with money and could not make himself think about what was happening – he allowed events to overtake him. It seemed that all his difficulties were encapsulated in this muddle: the ambivalence regarding therapy; the difficulty about giving and receiving; honesty and straightforwardness in relationships; how to express mixed feelings; and last but most important, letting things happen rather than thinking about them, action not understanding. Of course this was just what I had done when I set the lower fee. I had acted rather than understood, and the returned cheque, together with the offer of paying me through a third party, his wife, had echoes of how I had been influenced by a third party in the setting of the fee. Had I stuck to my usual charge, I might have allowed Matthew to have negative feelings about me and yet still have taken up the offer of regular meetings. Instead, thinking I was enabling him to have something which otherwise he might not have been able to afford, I had put Matthew in the very position he was telling me he so badly needed to understand and to avoid; that of the helpless victim who is too stupid to manage things for himself. I had wanted to help Matthew and had been accommodating in finding a time that suited him and a fee that he could manage. It was not intrinsically wrong for me to have tried to assist Matthew in these ways, but I should have understood his requests in terms of his own difficulties, rather than acting on emotions he stirred up in me. At last some of these things were beginning to come into the open and, as we talked about them, Matthew started to make connections with muddles regarding money, his own mixed feelings about our relationship, and how angry feelings had been avoided through my setting of the lower fee.

Just before a vacation break, Matthew told me that he would not be able to continue coming at his usual time, because a work placement he had to undertake clashed with the time he saw me. He was again worried about the financial outlay and whether he could really afford therapy. He talked about the placement with great feeling: it was too bad that it clashed with something he valued so much; he never seemed to have control over events; it was absolutely essential he did the placement and the authorities at work could not be expected to alter things for him. He ended by saying how disruptive he found all these changes in times. For a moment I was convinced that I would have to find a new time for Matthew and then I realized that yet again I was seeing him as utterly helpless, the victim of circumstance, someone who had to have allowances made for him.

It is pertinent to say here that I had already agreed to two one-off changes of times for individual sessions, and a change in the time of regular meetings when the training attendance day had been altered. With hindsight, I think the change in regular times was probably right but the two changes in individual sessions I should not have agreed to.

I decided that I must use my understanding and leave Matthew to manage things for himself. I said it sounded as if it had not been helpful of me to allow the times of our meetings to be altered and, although the situation he now described was difficult, I thought it would be better if we stuck to what we had agreed. After a long pause, Matthew sighed heavily and told me that in fact he did think he might be able to negotiate a different time with his boss at work regarding the placement. The fact that these difficulties had come up just before a break was also relevant: in talking about not continuing, Matthew was perhaps retaliating for what he felt powerless to alter, the interruption to our relationship through my vacation. However, to interpret solely on these grounds would be to ignore other factors and might have been experienced as a stereotypical therapist comment, retaliatory in itself, and humiliating.

In subsequent sessions Matthew was able to tell me how muddling he had found my lowering of the fee and how worrying it had been when I agreed to different times. His way of presenting himself was of someone who was extremely humble and excessively grateful to be seen at all, and yet this very humility and gratitude was a cover for very different feelings. Although I understood this intellectually, I still allowed myself to get caught up in making things easy for Matthew, rather than giving him the respect he deserved in treating him like any other client.

The whole issue of fees and whether they should be altered to meet particular circumstances is a vexed one. In public settings therapy may be subsidized, making it possible for individuals on low incomes or without incomes to receive therapeutic help. In a perfect situation the right fee would always be the one that the client is able to pay, and one that demonstrates an understanding of both external and internal realities. By this I mean that in terms of fees, as well as in other things, no two people are alike, even though they may apparently have the same amount of money and be in similar circumstances. Our early experiences of giving and receiving will be involved in how we feel about the fee: the best of therapists would determine what each person should pay through an understanding of what has gone before. In an initial consultation this is rarely possible, and in private practice therapists' needs – their valuing of themselves, the standard of living to which they aspire – are also factors that come into the setting of the fee. It is not just based on the client, and this is a reality that has to be worked with. Increasingly, in private practice, I think it is best to have a set fee and to stick to it. Unless you are willing, or able, to see individuals at a very low cost, I suspect the negotiation of the fee, when we are talking of the very small amounts which are usually involved, probably does not make much difference purely in financial terms. The meaning is much more to do with how it feels to be asked to pay a fixed amount and then for this agreement to be adhered to. I am not suggesting that the fee should never be altered but in the example I have just given I now realize that there were no real external reasons for a lower fee. My decision to alter my charge was based on feelings stirred up in me by the referrer and the client, together with my desire to be the right person for both.

In the next example, the feelings stirred up in the therapist were again the trigger for an alteration, rather than an understanding of what was behind the request for a lower charge.

MELANIE: TRYING TO BE PERFECT

The client, whom I will call Melanie, had been in therapy before but it had stopped, either because she had decided not to continue or because her therapist had moved away. I was never sure of the precise details. Melanie was married and had a little girl who was now almost a year old. Some hours after the birth of her daughter, Melanie was told that she had a genetic handicap which would severely restrict her learning capacity. At the beginning of her time with me Melanie talked and talked, hardly drawing breath between her utterances. I was aware of two feelings in myself – first exhaustion, and second a feeling of admiration for this young woman and the way in which she was coping with the disappointment of having a child who was not 'perfect'. Melanie was a 'good' client in the sense that she always came on time, left as soon as I indicated the session was over, paid promptly and caused me no particular anxiety other than a sense that she was presenting herself as she thought she ought to be rather than as she truly was. I understood this in terms of Melanie's difficulties, the need to be acceptable and to manage everything, including anxiety, for herself. I was also aware that the way in which she was coping was too good to be true. She threw herself into being a perfect mother and was determined her daughter would be 'normal'. Indeed the care she lavished on her baby paid dividends, with the result that doctors, health visitors, friends and family, were all 'amazed' at the progress little Sally was making. It is relevant to say here that this situation touched closely on events that had occurred in my own life, events of which I was fully aware and knew must be kept out of my relationship with Melanie.

About ten months passed and gradually Melanie seemed able to relax and did not talk so compulsively. She was also able to begin to acknowledge the distress she felt about Sally's condition, and the terrible disappointment of not having the child she had wanted. For the first time she admitted the limitations to her daughter's potential, how she would never be able to fend for herself and what this meant to Melanie and her husband. It was at this point that my objectivity got lost and I ceased to be empathic but became sympathetic and over-involved.

One day Melanie told me that this would have to be her last session as it had become impossible for her to go on paying my fee. Her husband was to have his hours reduced and the family budget could no longer stretch to include the cost of her therapy. I had been aware that she sometimes talked about financial difficulties but I also knew that there was ample evidence of enough money, if not a lot. Nevertheless, all this knowledge got lost and instead of waiting to see what else Melanie had to say, I immediately intervened by saying that it seemed she felt there was no possibility of talking about the financial difficulties, or of me being able to understand them. Perhaps if I had not included the word 'financial', I would not have carried on with the series of mistakes that followed, as this would at least have left the way open for a wider interpretation of what the difficulties were. I think Melanie probably heard my comment as something like this: 'How can you not see that I am a good and sympathetic therapist. Tell me about your problems and I will solve them for you.' Indeed this was how I wanted her to see me. How could I refuse help to a young woman who was so courageously coping with a child who caused her such worries? Of course this was not the issue at all as Melanie's difficulties were rooted in the past. She had sought therapy long before Sally's birth and I should have known that the help she needed from me was understanding, not action. Instead of empathizing with her situation and using this understanding to facilitate Melanie's feelings, I identified (saw myself in her and her in me) and sympathized with her predicament. I now felt I could and should make up for the distress she was experiencing, by demonstrating that she meant more to me than mere money.

This is a tricky situation for the therapist but I now know that what I did was unhelpful. But what should I have done? First of all I should simply have waited to see what came up and taken my cues from the evidence that was presented. If this did not become apparent immediately, I could have postponed any alteration by saying something like this: 'You have told me you can no longer afford my fee, but rather than stopping straight away I wonder whether you would like to consider continuing our work together so that we can keep on talking about this matter.' In this situation Melanie might have said, 'But I know I can't pay your fee.' I could then have said I was prepared to accept this for the moment but that the problem was one we could keep on discussing. In this way I would have been keeping options open, Melanie would know I was concerned with understanding rather than solely with money, and that I was prepared to take the risk of her not paying. There was also the possibility of increased understanding of the difficulty, which might or might not have been about the fee. With further exploration I would have been in a better position to know what to do.

What actually happened was that I immediately said: 'You seem to feel the fee is more important to me than you are and that it is impossible to talk about this.' My statement was not entirely wrong, but instead of allowing time to explore her response, which was at a practical level of household budgets, I became caught up in my own feelings of guilt and rushed in with my next intervention. I suggested Melanie should tell me what she thought she could afford. I had now blocked any anger she might have regarding my fee, and by suggesting that the ground rules could be altered so easily I had also demonstrated that the firm container for feelings was in fact extremely shaky. Melanie responded with a manifest statement of relief and gratitude – she had never imagined I would be so kind. However, her confusion was also apparent, and she had no idea how to arrive at an acceptable amount. Melanie sounded worried and upset. This demonstrates how anxiety-provoking it is to have a therapist who hands over responsibility to the client, but I was blind to everything except my need to be kind to this young woman. I suggested that she talk to her husband and let me know the following week what they had decided so that we could discuss it further. Melanie's discomfort must have been acute. She now had a therapist who was quite unable to keep firm boundaries, had abdicated all responsibility, and had now put her in charge.

After this session was over I began to appreciate what I had done, but I did not know how to remedy the errors. I tried to rationalize the situation by arguing with myself that being too rigid about fees was unhelpful, for surely therapists must take into account the real world in which money was short and which presented individuals with impossible choices. I was deeply concerned but still unable to see how to resolve matters in a way that was really helpful to my client.

The following week Melanie arrived still embarrassed and awkward. She and her husband had discussed the fee and had carefully worked out their budget. It took a long time before she could tell me the sum they had arrived at. It was just half my original fee. When she told me the amount, I was stunned and immediately aware that I felt angry. I had been assuming the reduction would be a small one and when it was not in line with my thinking, I felt undervalued and taken for granted. I knew I must not speak until I had sorted out my own position but I also realized these feelings were going to interfere with any subsequent work. There seemed little I could do as I had given Melanie respon- sibility for determining the fee, she had done what I had asked and now I was stuck with it. Doubtless Melanie must have registered my dis-ease, at an unconscious level if not a conscious one, and as she began to talk about other matters, I tried to sort out my own feelings knowing that I would have to address the matter of the fee again.

Having made this decision I started to listen more carefully to what Melanie was saying. I heard that the previous week she had attended her aerobics class but had been unable to participate because of back pain. The teacher had spoken to her after the class and had suggested Melanie call round to her home, as she thought she might be able to offer further help. Melanie did so and the teacher offered her individual exercise classes in her own home 'at such a ridiculously low cost, I couldn't believe it', she told me. Melanie had felt uncomfortable. It did not seem professional and she wondered what was in it for the aerobics teacher, and why she should want to single her out. She had decided not to take up the offer. There was a pause and then Melanie said she did not know what to say next, for she felt disconnected. I took this as my cue and said that I thought she might be picking up something disconnected in me, in that I had not been attending to her properly. I went on to say that although I had agreed to what she and her husband had decided, I felt she was telling me that this abdication of responsibility had been un- helpful to her. She had said she felt uncomfortable with the offer her teacher had made and it seemed she must be wondering why I had agreed to lower my fee, and what was in it for me.

Melanie's first comment was a manifest one. She spoke of dis- appointment that I seemed to be retracting my kind offer and I imme- diately felt guilty and anxious. When we feel anxious most of us try to discharge this unpleasant feeling and this is just what I did. Thinking honesty was the best policy I told Melanie that I had been surprised at the amount she had suggested, that half the original fee was, I thought, too low. Just as I had been about to move back into the therapist role, I again became the client using Melanie to relieve my feelings. I sensed that she was extremely angry but her voice was controlled as she told me how shocked she was by what I had said. Really the amount she had proposed was more than she could afford. She had been going to ask her mother to pay for the sessions but when they had last met her mother had spoken of shares which had not yielded what had been expected, so she could not look to help from this source. Melanie went on to talk about dire financial straits and as I listened I felt more and more guilty and upset at the mess I had created. It was nearing the end of the session when Melanie told me that she did not think she could come back the following week. I knew I must give myself time for reflection and not rush in with any more unhelpful comments or interpretations. Therefore I simply said that I hoped she would return so that we could keep on talking about the fee and what had happened. When she left I felt wretched and throughout the following week I worried about my client and became convinced she would never return.

When Melanie arrived for the next session, she looked pale and her manner was hostile and angry. She said she had had a terrible time and did not see how she could go on seeing me. There was a long silence and then she told me that she been so angry that when she got home she had telephoned a friend and told her all about the fee and what I had said. Melanie had been amazed to discover that her friend thought her anger was quite justified. This was communicated in a very defensive tone as if I would contradict her. I said that I was not surprised she was angry at the way I had managed things. It must have seemed confusing and upsetting. First of all I had agreed to lower the fee without trying to understand what it meant, next I had given her the task of deciding how much she should pay, and, when she had done what I asked, I had told her I was disappointed with the sum proposed. She must feel thoroughly fed up. 'Do you mean it was your fault?' she asked. I said that I did not think I had managed things in a way that was helpful to her.

Melanie now told me that after the conversation with her friend she had felt much better but the next day she had again become convinced that everything was her fault, not mine. There was a long silence which was finally broken by Melanie beginning to cry. She said that she could not believe I had confirmed her feelings by admitting my errors. There was another silence and then she told me she was remembering how her father would go on and on about his troubles to her. She had been frightened and had not known how to respond. Her father would get in a terrible rage, Melanie would feel uncontrollably angry herself, but the only way she felt she could really get back at him was to sit in silence and refuse to show her anger. This must have been how she experienced the previous session when I intruded my difficulties into her therapy, a space that was hers and for which she was paying. Melanie experienced anger but presented a calm and controlled front.

The issue of the fee was still not resolved and I did not mange to sort it out properly until some weeks later. When we spoke about it in the session I am describing, I fell into another trap, that of taking control. I became so concerned with taking back the responsibility I had abandoned, I again forgot to listen to my client and be guided by what she said. I told Melanie that having agreed to a lower fee I felt it was right to stick to this for the time being but we could review the situation before the summer break, which was due in two months. Although Melanie expressed satisfaction with this arrangement I was to learn subsequently that it was not what was required.

Two sessions later Melanie told me that she would have to miss her appointment the following week as she was going on holiday. A relative was going to pay for this and she had felt worried about telling her father about the arrangement. When she had spoken to him she had pretended the holiday was being paid for by her husband. Her father was feckless and irresponsible but she still felt concern for him and was afraid he would be hurt by the thought of not being able to provide for her what her aunt could. Melanie feared her father would 'have a go' at her because she was always telling him how hard up she was and he might think this was untrue if he knew she was being taken away to the sun and the sea. I said that I wondered if it was also difficult for her to talk to me about this because I had been irresponsible in the way I managed money matters. Yes, she had felt worried about it. Now that she was paying less she felt beholden to me, she felt guilty and kept on thinking she would like to bake me a cake or give me a gift. I said that it sounded as if the lower fee was unhelpful, and that it made her feel patronized and in my power, which resulted in her not being able to bring all her feelings into the relationship. Melanie now told me that she had been worried about the cancelled session the following week. She knew I charged for missed appointments but she had remembered that her previous therapist did not ask her to pay if she gave a week's notice. She had forgotten what I did in these circumstances. I said that I did charge for missed or cancelled appointments. There was a short pause. 'Yes, I do remember you saying that.' Melanie then told me she was in the process of getting herself a part-time job involving children and that when she returned from her holiday she could go back to paying the full fee.

At last I had been firm and now we almost had the framework re-established. I was someone who could be trusted to look after Melanie's childlike feelings, just as she had found inner resources to look after children herself, and to pay for her therapy. If only I had been able to wait and see and be guided by the clues this client gave me, I might never have got into what was almost an irretrievable situation. Nevertheless, the fact I was able, albeit very late in the day, to see what was required, enabled Melanie to continue working with her difficulties. I have no doubt at all that, although she might have remained in therapy with me for a time out of gratitude and dependence, the lower fee would have resulted in Melanie dropping out, as the new arrangement increasingly inhibited the expression of her feelings. She had accurately perceived me as someone who could not cope with her anger but preferred to put her in a dependent position, so that her difficulties could not be worked through. Only when this was acknowledged and the frame re-established could the therapeutic relationship be maintained.

SARAH: A LOSS OF AUTHORITY

In this last example the client, whom I will call Sarah, contacted me initially to refer someone else. The referral came to nothing and some months later Sarah rang to ask whether I would see her, because as she put it she wanted some very short-term help. Sarah was an administrator who also did some counselling herself. During the initial consultation it became apparent that she and I both knew someone with whom she had worked in the past. At first I thought this might be a reason for not seeing Sarah, but as the colleague we had in common no longer lived in the area, and I had no further contact with her although Sarah still had occasional meetings, I decided this was not an obstacle. Regular meetings were accepted and I made it clear that I charged for missed or cancelled sessions.

From the start Sarah was ambivalent regarding her relationship with me. She made it plain that she was doubtful about therapy and the wisdom of stirring up the past. Sessions felt awkward, there were long silences, difficulties about keeping appointments due to other commitments, and, hardest of all, a feeling that Sarah wanted me to talk with her about her problems in an intellectual discourse, colleague to colleague, rather than allowing me to know her in a more direct way. Occasionally, Sarah's extremely professional and controlled front slipped and I was allowed to glimpse the frightened child who had always had to manage everything, no matter how great the cost to herself. It seemed that when this happened Sarah became frightened by the feelings stirred up in her and would retreat back into her capable, managing role. I was very moved by the little Sarah let me know of her sad and lonely childhood and moved also by her dignity and reserve.

Very soon after I began seeing her, Sarah told me that she would not be able to come the following week as she had a prior commitment. There was a long silence, broken by Sarah explaining how she had to attend an important case meeting which involved several professional colleagues. This was said in a cool, rather detached manner and I could feel my own anxiety rising as to what I should do. I knew it was possible for me to see her at another time and instead of waiting to see whether this possibility would occur to Sarah, or simply accepting the fact that she had decided to attend a work meeting rather than see me, I suggested an alternative time.

In fact I was frightened of Sarah and intimidated by the extremely rational way in which she presented herself. My offer stemmed from anxiety that I would be made to appear foolish if I tried to understand what her request meant in terms other than the rational. Sarah accepted my offer with gratitude but a few months later I was told that after the coming vacation break she would be taking an extra holiday and would have to miss two of her appointments. Now I knew I had made the ground rules quite clear but at this stage in my work I still found it hard to stay with what intellectually I knew was right, when emotionally it felt so unfair and difficult. Sarah was older than me, she was a competent and extremely professional woman, articulate, knowledgeable and sophisticated. She still had contact with someone I knew, another professionally high-powered individual and one who was extremely sceptical about psychotherapy. Sarah herself often made me feel gauche and silly. She would say, sarcastically, 'Of course you won't tell me that, it's not allowed,' or 'I know what you'll say, it's what I say to people.' Although I knew these remarks were defensive and that Sarah was trying to turn me into a colleague rather than a therapist, I felt my own belief in my ability to help was being undermined. Of course it was but this is not a cue for therapists to change their ways of working, but simply an example of the client trying to deal with feelings of dependency, needs that have to be understood, not avoided.

Already I had made the first mistake in giving an unasked-for change of time and now I went on to make a series of mistakes that eventually led to Sarah ending our relationship. I did not charge her for the two missed sessions when she took her holiday. This was not referred to by Sarah and she kept on coming, but as the summer holiday approached she told me that she had decided to take up a place on a course and that this would clash with the time she saw me. I tried to understand this in terms of the vacation interruption and Sarah's ambivalence about dependency, which was partially accepted but with such sarcasm it felt difficult to feel my interpretation was anything other than the hackneyed and obvious comment all therapists would make. I said that I did not think it would be helpful to change her time and Sarah told me she would return to see me for our first meeting after the break but it might be to say that she had decided not to continue.

After the summer when we met again Sarah told me that she did want to go on seeing me but not on a weekly basis, as she felt this was too much, and proposed fortnightly meetings. Once again I tried to understand what Sarah was asking for as an expression of her ambivalence, which again was accepted at a manifest level but still she insisted this was what she wanted. I told her that I was unable to see her on this basis and she asked me why. I asked whether she had any thoughts about my reasons. Sarah replied by telling me she assumed that a two-weekly slot would be hard to fill but since I had been accommodating over altering her times in the past, she thought I might be willing to consider this proposal. I said that I thought it had not been helpful to her when I had offered her alternative times and had not charged her for the two sessions when she had been on holiday. 'Why do you say that?' she asked. 'Well, in our initial meeting I think I made it clear to you what the arrangements would be and yet I did not stick to what I said. This must have made you feel worried about me, about my trustworthiness and my ability to offer you something safe and secure.' Sarah looked at me very directly. 'Yes, I was puzzled. You were extremely clear and I liked that. I thought you might be frightened of me when you did not charge me when I went away.' Her perception was accurate. 'So it has been your feeling that I am frightened of you and my inconsistency which has made you decide not to continue.' Sarah agreed that these were factors in her decision, although she felt she had learnt a lot about herself and wanted to return the following week for a final meeting. This she did and I think it was true that her contact with me had not been a total failure, but there is no doubt that my inability to stay with the framework for therapy I had proposed in our first meeting was the main factor in Sarah terminating the contact.

From the therapist's viewpoint, asking clients to pay for missed sessions is one of the hardest aspects of the frame to maintain, particularly in private practice. In a public setting, as I have suggested in an earlier chapter, if clients are expected to pay for missed or cancelled appointments then the feelings this engenders can be projected into the institution. It is not the therapist who is insisting on payment but the organization. Changes of time are not so easily accommodated and again the firmness of the frame can be seen as external to the therapeutic relationship. In theory, the therapist might agree to extra sessions or alteration in times but the complexity of arrangements necessary in a public setting make this impossible. This may make for a more comfortable relationship but it is in fact just these difficult feelings about firmness and consistency which are a crucial part of the work itself. When just client and therapist, and nobody else, are involved, then feelings about paying for missed sessions or rearranging appointments have to be dealt with by them, and there is less scope for projection.

Individual therapists will develop their own way of working and decide for themselves whether missed sessions are paid for, whether appointments can be rearranged and what to do about holidays which do not coincide with their own arrangements. Whatever you decide to do, the important thing is to state it clearly and then try to stick to what has been agreed. I have had to learn this lesson over and over again and I know that I will have to go on learning from my mistakes. Some clients seem to accept with ease the arrangements we make, but it is helpful to bear in mind that it may be just as much part of one individual's pathology that they cause you no anxieties regarding the frame, as it is part of another's that they constantly try to break boundaries. The person who always comes exactly on time, leaves when you say the session is over and pays the bill regularly, is in just as much need of having feelings understood as the person who does not. The compliant client may be so frightened of the consequences of not doing these things that they become meaningless rituals, adhered to because a higher authority has imposed a set of rules, which have nothing to do with the client as an individual but are there to serve the therapist.

When you find yourself wanting to alter the framework, it is necessary to think about what is being stirred up, both in terms of your own difficulties and the client's. In my experience, when I find I have got into a muddle with a particular individual, it is usually because the difficulties that have brought the client into therapy have touched on some area of difficulty in myself. Another factor that can cause problems is when there is some connection between the client and myself, the referrer or a mutual colleague. When an individual is referred by another worker this can make therapists feel much is expected of them, so that the way in which the frame is established is not simply about therapist and client, but is made with a third party in mind. In Matthew's case, when it came to a discussion of the fee and regular appointments I remembered what the referrer had told me, that is, that there were financial difficulties. Matthew also told me money was a problem but nothing he said really indicated that he could not pay my usual charge.

With Melanie, although there was no third party influencing what I did, my own unresolved feelings about a personal matter were allowed to intrude into her therapy. With Sarah, although I had thought my past contact with a mutual colleague would cause no problems, I became concerned with the possibility that my failure to accommodate would be seen as harsh and uncaring, both by Sarah and by the third party known to us both.

It is probable that at some point in the therapy the frame will become shaky or broken but this will not be disastrous if the error can be understood and rectified. Perhaps the biblical reference to the love of money being the root of all evil is an apt way to close this chapter. Money in itself is not evil. It is necessary to earn money in order to live and it is a way of valuing ourselves and of valuing others. In the therapeutic relationship it provides us with a fertile source of understanding. It is the love of money for its own sake that can wreak havoc in human relationships. The sensitive therapist must always strive to understand what the financial transaction means for each individual client, whilst maintaining a firm framework in which these meanings can unfold.

Chapter 9

A brief intervention

Teaching on a counselling course, I have found that students tend to see long-term therapy as superior to short contacts and I think this view may have three main sources, all of them stemming from anxiety. One is that psychoanalysis is seen as the peak of a hierarchy of therapeutic interventions, and thus to work short-term is seen as inferior, a blow to the therapist's self-esteem. The second stems from a belief that given enough time all problems can be resolved, and therefore brief contacts stir up anxieties regarding limitations. It is difficult to accept that no relationship, however long it may continue, can provide the answers to all difficulties. Third, and even more fundamental, may be the anxiety that is stirred up through the idea of two people becoming important to each other, and having to manage these feelings in an encounter that takes place within a set period of time. It is true that for many people, particularly those with severe problems, even a partial resolution will not be achieved unless there is an opportunity for their difficulties to be understood gradually. However, in some cases it may be possible for change to occur in brief contacts, and in this chapter I want to describe a piece of short-term work, just six sessions, with a young woman who came to see me because she suffered anxiety attacks.

KAREN: THE IMPORTANCE OF FLEXIBILITY

I received a telephone call from a counsellor, who told me that she had been approached by someone, whom I will call Mrs White, because her daughter aged 24 needed help. The counsellor explained to me that there had been a misunderstanding regarding the location of her practice and that the travelling distance involved made it impossible for the young woman to come to see her. I was told that Mrs White had specifically asked for a Christian counsellor, because her daughter was a keen member of the local church, and the whole family shared Christian values. The counsellor did not ask whether I fulfilled this criterion, so I simply said I was willing for my name to be given to Mrs White. After this short conversation I started to think about my potential client and wondered about her mother's involvement. Was the wish for counselling a result of the daughter's need or the mother's? Who was it that really wanted a Christian counsellor, Mrs White or her daughter? Who would contact me, parent or child? Already, even before knowing what the difficulty was, I was alerted to the possibility that there might be problems regarding mothers and daughters.

A few days later I heard from the daughter, whom I will call Karen, who simply asked for a consultation, nothing being said about her mother initiating the contact or about me being a Christian. Karen was an attractive young woman, slim and athletic in build. At first she appeared confident and composed but as soon as she sat down and started to speak I was aware of anxiety. 'I get panic attacks, I don't know why. I really don't see how you can help. Do you think you can?' Karen's words came out in a rush and seemed to demand an immediate response. 'It seems as if this situation is difficult and is making you feel panicky,' I said. 'Yes it is,' Karen responded, 'My mother thinks I ought to see a counsellor but I really don't know whether it's what I want.'

I was keeping the focus on what was happening in the room, not deflecting it by asking questions or providing answers, as this would have moved us away from emotional states into the realm of knowing and of intellect. By acknowledging the panic I was trying to contain Karen's fears so that she could experience me as someone who was not frightened by anxiety. Her statement, 'My mother thinks I ought to see a counsellor but I really don't know whether it's what I want,' gave a clue as to what the anxiety might be about, that is, having feelings that were different from her mother's. I did not want to say whether I could help at this stage because it is more important for people to experience therapists as helpful than to be given statements about their ability to help.

What I said next was, 'Perhaps we can use the time today for you to decide whether or not you would like to see me on a regular basis.' I was trying to separate Karen from her mother and to discover who wanted what. Karen seemed to relax slightly as she thought about this but then I could see the anxiety returning when she said, 'I don't know what to say. What would you like to know?' This is always difficult, because if you ask a series of questions, while it may alleviate anxiety, it will also result in the therapist determining what is talked about rather than discovering what is important to the client. I responded in a typically therapist sort of way by saying, 'Perhaps you could tell me something about yourself.' 'Well,' said Karen, 'I work in finance. I've got a good job and I play a lot of badminton. What else do you want to know?' This was said rather aggressively, as if Karen felt my invitation was crass but could not bring herself to say so. At this point I was aware of feeling somewhat anxious myself because of her hostility, but rather than getting drawn into the anxiety, either by retaliation or submission, I tried to think about what was going on.

I thought this situation might be familiar, that Karen needed someone to tell her what to say before she could feel herself on safe ground. Perhaps it was only when she knew what the expectations of the other were that she would know how to proceed. It might also be that this had something to do with her panic attacks. There could be conflict involved in always trying to meet others' expectations, as these might conflict with Karen's needs. It could be she needed to have an experience of finding out what she wanted, but it was this very situation that provoked the anxiety. As I struggled with these thoughts, I knew that it was important to stay with what she had said. Karen may only have given a couple of facts about herself but what she chose to say must be important.

'You've told me you've got a good job and that you play badminton. I wonder if you could tell me a little more about these two things.' Karen now spoke at some length. She told me she had not done well at school, and had in fact been expelled because of bad behaviour. She had felt angry with the school for not recognizing her abilities and, after a confused period of feeling herself to be a disruptive and upsetting influence in the family, had gone on to further education and a training in administration. Karen told me that she was very good at her job but sometimes felt angry with colleagues who were not as efficient as she; these frustrations were not expressed to her workmates. She loved playing badminton, had achieved a very high standard, and in fact was soon going to take part in an important tournament. As she talked about badminton I was aware that Karen relaxed and spoke with excitement and animation. I commented that her sport was obviously very important to her. She seemed pleased I had recognized this fact and said that it was the one thing she seemed able to do really well. She was very proud that, because of her skill, she was often asked to play in the men's games. I thought about sport and badminton in particular, about how you need to be aggressive to play well, and how Karen delighted in this activity. I wondered about aggression and competitive feelings but did not put my thoughts into words at this stage.

Karen appeared more relaxed and when she had finished telling me of her work and leisure, she said that she had assumed I would want to hear about her childhood and her family. 'I don't want to talk about that. Everyone assumes problems come from your past.' 'So it was important to you that I didn't ask what you thought I would?' I replied. Karen sighed, 'Yes, my parents are marvellous. They have done so much for me. I couldn't ask for better parents.' I said, 'It's important for me to know that?' 'Yes,' replied Karen, 'whatever problems I've got they aren't to do with them. I was adopted and everyone always thinks this must cause problems, that you must be curious, that you must want to know about your mother. I have no interest whatsoever in finding out about my mother.' I was being told quite explicitly that I must not trespass into these forbidden areas and if they were to be explored it must be at Karen's pace, not mine.

We were now over half-way through this first meeting and I decided to introduce the possibility of regular meetings. I said something like this: 'I wonder if at this stage it might be helpful for us to talk about you coming to see me on a regular basis?' Karen told me she would like to come but did not want to commit herself to anything long-term. I asked what she had in mind and she said about five or six sessions, possibly fewer. I suggested we arrange six appointments and that she could tell me if she wanted to bring the meetings to an end before that. This was agreed.

In the ensuing meetings we followed a pattern similar to the first consultation. Karen's anxiety would be severe when she first arrived and I felt that at any moment she might take flight and rush out of the room. She wished I would ask questions, did not know what to say, had told me all there was to tell, and, even if there was more, could not see how talking would help. This stirred up anxiety in me regarding my own abilities as a therapist, which I knew needed to be contained as they were just the feelings Karen was unable to manage in herself. I would acknowledge how difficult it must feel that I did not do what she wanted, and then very gradually Karen would relax and start to talk about herself.

I learnt that she had an older sister, also adopted, and a younger sister, who was the natural daughter of her parents. This younger sister had a physical disability which resulted in the whole family having to make allowances for her. Karen told me more about her expulsion from school and how she had gone around with a 'bad crowd', a period that had involved truancy and alcohol. She had felt, and still felt, desperately guilty for the upset she had caused her parents at this time. Karen was now living away from home and had a boyfriend who was very important to her. She was worried that he might end their relationship, although she said there was no evidence for this fear.

All this information was imparted in a factual way, emotion being expressed only as each brief communication was finished, when Karen would become anxious and tell me that she couldn't see how any of these things could be connected with her panic attacks. I tried to make connections for her, suggesting that the suppression of all her angry feelings and the anxiety she experienced might be related. This interpretation was not accepted. Karen told me that she did not feel angry, that the disruptive behaviour had been the result of her badness. The fear that her boyfriend might leave and her willingness to do whatever he wanted, Karen insisted, was essential, as that was how you had to behave if you wanted to keep a relationship going. My interpretation was both premature and incorrect. Although triggered by current events, Karen's anxiety would not originate in the present, but was more likely to have its source in much earlier experiences of fusion and separation. My intervention stemmed from anxiety in myself, stirred up by a need to provide explanations for the feelings that were so frightening to Karen.

I realized that any thinking I might do regarding the source of Karen's anxiety should not be shared with her. This was an important factor in our relationship and I began to work out why this might be so. First of all I had to free myself from Karen – the fact that she didn't want to make connections did not mean I couldn't. I allowed myself to think about being adopted, of how it might feel to have a younger sister with a physical disability, of how Karen might feel about it given her own athletic prowess. I imagined Karen being curious about her origins, of what this might mean to her and what she might think it would mean to her adoptive parents. I wondered about becoming adolescent and how necessary it is to move away from parents, to find your own values, your own way of living. This is difficult for any young person but how much harder might it be if you are adopted and have been given so much? I thought about badminton and the freedom it must give to express aggression, to be competitive, to be yourself. As Karen talked I allowed myself to have all these thoughts, but I remembered that for the moment she could not allow herself the freedom of thinking as I did. I was not sure at this stage whether Karen was going to be able to find for herself the reason for her panic attacks, nor indeed whether my hypothesis that they probably stemmed from very early experiences of attachment and separation was correct.

In our fourth meeting Karen started by telling me that she had had a panic attack the previous week. Her boyfriend had suggested they go out one evening and had asked Karen where she would like to go. She said she didn't mind, so he opted for a meal in a restaurant. Karen told me that in fact she really wanted to go to the cinema. The problem was, she said, that she only knew what she wanted when her boyfriend said what he wanted. By this time Karen could not state her wish because it was in opposition with what she now perceived as her boyfriend's wish. To oppose him, she felt, would result in conflict, conflict which would eventually cause him to end their relationship. They went out for a meal and she had a panic attack in the restaurant.

The cause of her anxiety was now much clearer. Karen did not recognize her own needs and was confused about what she wanted for herself. She looked to others for guidance and only when she knew what they wanted could she begin to know about her own desires. With this knowledge came an awareness of the separateness of the other and the probability, for Karen, of abandonment if she did not suppress her own needs. The possibility of two people with conflicting needs being able to find a way out of this dilemma, without one abandoning the other, was not within Karen's experience. The anger that must have been a part of always giving in to others, and the anxiety which must have resulted from the fear of rejection, simmered away until it came out in a panic attack. Although I had not thought all this through in quite the way it is presented here, in the session I was able to formulate something along these lines. I could not see, however, that presenting an intellectual explanation of Karen's problem was going to help her resolve the dilemma, so I said nothing.

After talking about her boyfriend and how important he was to her, Karen told me that because the badminton tournament had been rearranged and now clashed with the time she saw me, she would be unable to attend the following week's meeting. In the initial consultation, I had explained that I would be reserving the agreed time for Karen until she told me she no longer wanted it, and would be asking her to pay for all the sessions that were arranged. This had been accepted and when Karen told me that she would be unable to come the following week, she said, 'I suppose I will have to pay even though I can't come.' It would have been easy to say that this was not necessary – indeed this was what I wanted to say and it felt extremely hard to say anything else. However, because Karen had told me that she felt she had to meet other people's expectations, I felt it was important not to act on my feeling – the desire to go along with what she wanted – since this was probably Karen's feeling which was being projected into me. Therefore what I said was this: 'We agreed these sessions be reserved for you. There are still two meetings left, one of which you cannot now make. I wonder what you think it is right to do?' Karen flushed and said very angrily,

'Yes, I did agree so I suppose it's right that I pay. I don't feel very happy about it though. I think perhaps I'll make this the last meeting.' I said that this would mean we would only have had four meetings in all, and although this might be what she wanted to do, it did not sound as if it was really satisfactory. 'No,' said Karen, 'I don't really want to finish today, but what else can I do?' I thought for a moment and then said, 'It seems as if you and I are in a situation where you feel I am imposing something on you. This makes you angry and there seem to be only two things you can do. One is to give in and the other is to leave without having your final session. I wonder if together we might find a resolution which satisfies us both?' Karen was clearly moved by my words and burst into tears. When she was more composed she said, 'I thought you would just make me do what you wanted.'

We then discussed various alternatives and it became quite clear that, although Karen would have to miss the fifth meeting, she did want the time of the sixth and final session kept open for her. We agreed she should pay half her fee for the missed session and that we would meet the following week for the last one. After these negotiations, Karen was able to tell me that this discussion had been tremendously important to her. She went on to say how difficult it was to have a view different from that of her mother. When Karen felt herself at variance with her mother it always felt like a battle which one or other of them either lost or won, and in which there was no possibility of compromise. Towards the end of the session she told me how worried she was about having a panic attack when she went away for the badminton tournament. It was being held in another country and involved the visiting team living in the homes of their hosts. Karen felt she would have to fit in with the family and their expectations. She liked to have time on her own and she feared they might want her to accompany them on the excursions which were to be arranged.

When she returned two weeks later for our final meeting Karen told me that the visit had been a great success. She had thoroughly enjoyed it. She had not had a panic attack and had found time both to be on her own and to go out with the family. On her return she had thought a lot about her relationship with her boyfriend and had become aware that she was not sure she wanted to marry him. Karen then talked about her mother and how she knew she had to find a new way of relating to her, which did not mean having to tell her every detail of her life. She had gone to see her parents at the weekend and her mother had wanted to know where she had bought the new outfit she was wearing, how much it had cost and why she hadn't bought the suit her mother liked. Karen had been able to respond in a kindly way but without going into all the details. She said that her mother had seemed a bit surprised but not as hurt as Karen thought she would be. This had led her into thinking about her family and for the first time Karen told me that she did sometimes wonder where her physical characteristics had come from. She had thought she might be the result of a 'one night stand', an idea that was extremely upsetting. Karen wondered about her own ability to be a mother. She liked children and they liked her. She thought that perhaps one day she would have a child of her own. As we came to the end of our time Karen told me that she felt rather puzzled about counselling. She was not at all sure how talking about things helped, and she was quite sure she didn't want any more for the moment but would like to know that she could be in touch again if she wanted to.

When I thought about Karen after she had left and tried to evaluate what had been achieved, I was left with many unanswered questions. What would happen to the relationship with her boyfriend and with her family? Would she go on being curious about her origins, and where might this curiosity lead? Would she still have panic attacks? I had already begun to wonder whether Karen had been projecting her own doubts about commitment on to her boyfriend. She had been very clear about not making a long-term commitment to me and it may be that, because of her own experience of the mother who gave her up for adoption, Karen needed to feel in control of our relationship. It seemed she was now able to take back some of these projections and be in touch with her own rejecting feelings, explicitly *vis à vis* her boyfriend, and implicitly with me. There was some evidence that Karen was becoming able to form a more adult relationship with her mother, one in which she was able to keep things to herself. This too she had been able to do with me. I had not asked questions but had allowed Karen to determine what was talked about. I had respected her autonomy, and although this had resulted in anxiety we had managed to stay in a relationship. Only at the very end of our time together had Karen allowed me to know that she was curious about her origins. The forbidden area was still dangerous and painful, but it could now be acknowledged as relevant, and the past as having meaning.

The most important part of our work together had taken place in the fourth meeting, when I had not insisted on Karen paying the full fee for the missed session. In this instance I had decided that a rigid adherence to the frame would be experienced by Karen as placing the rule before the individual. I felt it was important for her to know that I was able to negotiate and compromise, to understand how it felt to be her. I knew too that to waive the fee altogether, what I felt I wanted to do, would be unhelpful to Karen. If I had done so she would not have been able to show me how angry she felt, and it was this expression of a feeling which had hitherto been felt to be the precursor to abandonment, that was most helpful to Karen. Having been angry with me, she was increasingly able to entertain critical thoughts about her family, without becoming overwhelmed with guilt.

In brief therapy therapists have to accept that their interventions may only lay the foundations for change, but of course this may equally well be true of longer-term work. Whether Karen will ever seek help again from me or from anyone else is not known. It may be she had got what she needed and it will be through her work, her badminton, and through living her life, with all its inevitable successes and failures, that Karen will find fulfilment. The therapeutic relationship is one way of working through personal difficulties, but not the only way. With young people in particular brief interventions may be helpful when there are problems about separation. Like parents therapists need to be able to let their clients go and to have confidence in their ability to manage life for themselves.

Chapter 10

Supervision

For therapists in training supervision is an integral part of their work, and even for those with experience another viewpoint can still inform and illuminate practice. The frame that has been advocated for the relationship between therapist and client holds true for that between supervisor and supervisee. For errors to be revealed, talked about and understood, an environment of privacy and trust is essential. The therapist is involved in the primary relationship with the client, the supervisor taking on a secondary role, that of supporting the main participants. As Casement (1990) has pointed out, we could see this as similar to the father's relationship with the mother and the child. Of course there may not be a man to perform this role, just as there may not be a woman to act as mother, and neither function should be seen simply in terms of gender. Nevertheless it is helpful for anyone, man or woman, who has sole responsibility for an infant, to have someone else who can support and help maintain the primary relationship of care. To avoid unnecessary confusion I will continue to refer to the 'someone else' in masculine terms.

The father who is able to put aside his own needs to give support to his partner in her relationship with the newborn child, allows the mother to be wholly available to her infant, free from external worries and anxieties. As the child develops there is another role for the father to play, that of helping the mother gradually to separate herself from the intense involvement she has had with the baby. Because he is not so closely identified with the infant, it is the father – representing the reality principle through his continuing connection with the outside world – who can increasingly allow external factors to impinge. Every mother and child relationship is unique, and there are no absolute rules for parenthood determining the right time, say, for infants to be left in the care of others, to be weaned, to begin nursery school or start sharing their toys; these are matters to be worked out in each individual family. It is through intuition and common sense, rather than from books and theory, that fathers play an important part in helping mothers decide what is best for each child. The wise supervisor, rather like the father, is able to provide a more objective view, and can help the supervisee maintain the relationship with the client when anxieties threaten.

In Chapters 1 and 6 I suggested that the ideal therapeutic relationship, like that between the mother and child, should be protected from outside interference. I also acknowledged that by talking about a case in supervision the contact was no longer entirely confidential. Unlike parents, however, therapists are not acting on instinct and intuition alone, although these may play their part in the therapeutic work. Their skills are developed through theoretical learning, their own personal experience of therapy, and through the help of a more objective third party, the supervisor. The supervisory relationship is similar to the therapeutic one. As the therapist provides containment and understanding for the client, so the supervisor performs the same function for the therapist, containing and understanding the feelings evoked in the affiliation with the client, thus protecting and maintaining the primary partnership.

When supervision is part of the therapist's training, the training body may require a report to be made, either verbally or in writing, so that the trainee's progress can be judged. If this should be the case, supervisors need to be aware of how their input may be experienced. It should be remembered that the anxiety which results from assessment can be a powerful block to learning.

I am now going to use two examples for illustration, one of them involving myself as supervisee and the other as supervisor. The first case, concerning a client whom I will call Susan, was one in which I was supervised by someone I had worked with for many years, a therapist I knew and trusted. I already had considerable experience, but knew that the feelings stirred up in me through my contact with this particular client needed to be talked about.

THERAPIST AS SUPERVISEE

The initial consultation had been conducted by a colleague working in the same agency. She had told Susan that she would be unable to see her on a regular basis, because she was expecting a baby and would soon be leaving the organization. This consultation had been discussed in a clinical meeting and my colleague spoke of her disappointment at not being able to see the client herself, because she had felt so drawn to the young woman, and how difficult it had been to tell Susan that this would not be possible. Some three months later I had a vacancy and I wrote offering regular appointments.

Susan was 22, an attractive, shy young woman, who evoked strong maternal feelings in me. She told me she suffered from attacks of anxiety, which did not seem to have any apparent cause, and it was this lack of a concrete reason for her feelings that frightened Susan so much. She felt as if there was something she did not know about herself, something hidden over which she had no control. She had a close and loving relationship with her boyfriend, who wanted them to become engaged, but Susan held back, unsure of whether she wanted to commit herself, and yet frightened that if she did not, she would lose him and only then know the full extent of her need. Susan told me, as she had my colleague, that she had been adopted when she was three months old, that her adoptive parents were loving and concerned, and she could not see how her adoption could have any connection with her present anxiety.

Once the facts of her life had been told, Susan lapsed into silence and sessions became difficult. She could not think of anything to say but unlike Karen, described in the previous chapter, Susan made no appeal to me for help, seeming to consider it her responsibility alone to keep the relationship going. I would sometimes break the silence to ask whether she felt stuck, whereupon Susan would smile shyly and attempt to respond. After this had happened fairly regularly I began to see that her response was for me, not because she had anything she really wanted to say. Then one day Susan told me of a situation in the office where she worked as a secretary. Susan did temporary work, not wanting to be employed on a permanent basis, as this might mean getting too involved. Although this was her choice, it also resulted in anxiety. She was intelligent and competent and knew that she was working below her capacity. She would have liked to stay in a job so that she could progress, but the pressures she experienced in attempting to fulfil her potential caused her to remain in a rather lowly position. Susan now described how sensitively she was attuned to the feelings of her work-mates. She recognized when they felt anxious and would try to respond in a way that would make them feel more comfortable. This, she said, she felt she did successfully but at great cost to herself, as she felt exhausted by her efforts. I recognized that this was what was happening in her relationship with me and I decided I must contain my desire to help Susan, so that she did not feel she had to speak to make me feel more comfortable.

After some weeks of sitting with the silence, making occasional eye contact and listening to Susan when she did speak, usually of her work or her relationship with her boyfriend, I was told something she had never told anyone else, that when she was eighteen she had traced her first mother, the woman who had given birth to her. Apparently this had been quite easy to do as she had been given the name and address, and with no real preparation Susan rang her mother, who agreed somewhat reluctantly to a meeting. This had been extremely distressing, as her mother made it clear that this was a one-off meeting and that she wanted no further contact. What made it even worse was that her mother had a friend with her so that an intimate conversation was impossible. All Susan discovered was that her father was an American, that she had been the result of a brief affair, and that her father did not even know of her existence. Her mother told her that this experience had made her determined never to marry or have any more children. It was at this point that Susan broke down and wept bitterly. Through her sobs she told me that she felt she had so damaged her mother that her life had been entirely blighted by Susan's birth. The meeting had been so distressing that Susan felt unable to tell anyone about it, her adoptive parents in particular, as she felt convinced that they would be desperately upset and hurt at what she had done.

We can now see how Susan's experiences might be reconstructed. After three months she had been separated from a mother, who, it seems reasonable to suppose, had extremely ambivalent feelings about her daughter. Superficially, her response to the meeting instigated by Susan appears to be rather harsh and uncaring, but it is likely that she was defending herself against what was probably an unbearable separation. The fact that she had to have a friend present suggests that Susan's mother could not allow herself to feel intimate again with the child she had relinquished all those years ago. We must not forget, however, that she did not refuse to see Susan, although of course she could have done. Twenty-two years ago a bewildered baby had been taken from her mother and then put into the care of an adoptive mother, who now had to learn to care for an infant already distressed by separation. We know that Susan is finely tuned to anxiety in others and we may guess that this sensitivity has been developed as a way of staying in relationships, but it results in Susan suppressing her own feelings. Her temporary work and fear of committing herself to her boyfriend were manifestations of Susan's need to protect herself against the possibility of rejection. Her contact with her first mother was an attempt to find out about the something she felt was hidden. But tragically all that the meeting did was to confirm the feeling that there was something in Susan which caused her mother to turn from her, something that had blighted her mother's life. Susan now felt she had confirmation that she had damaged her first mother, and believed that knowledge of her wish to know about her origins would damage her adoptive mother. We can now see how dangerous it must have felt to Susan to commit herself to an intimate relationship and the likelihood, if she could not resolve these problems, of her remaining on the edge of life.

In the next couple of months Susan started to speak more freely and began, at first very timidly, to wonder whether it was possible for babies to be influenced by what had happened to them. She had always thought tiny infants were in some way quite different from children and adults. The fact that they had no language, Susan imagined, meant they had no feelings. Gradually, she allowed herself to think it might not be quite like that, that perhaps babies did feel, that perhaps it might be quite hard for an infant to be separated from one mother and readjust herself to another.

One day she told me that she had spoken to her adoptive mother about the distressing meeting, and to Susan's amazement and relief her curiosity had been accepted and understood. The relationship had not been damaged, but indeed had deepened and become more intimate. Now just as our work was progressing so well and Susan was beginning to make real changes, I came to a decision of my own, namely to cease working for the organization at which I was seeing her. I was aware of extremely strong countertransference feelings towards Susan. She seemed to me like an ideal daughter, and it was hard to imagine anyone not wanting to care for her, and yet this was exactly what I was contemplating. It was at this point that I took the case to supervision, and of course the first thing that was pointed out to me was that the situation with me was not exactly the same as the situation Susan had faced in the past. I was not her mother but her therapist – something that seems quite obvious now but did not at the time.

This is an example of how important it is to have supervision, especially when you recognize strong involvement with a particular client. It is a situation that tends to occur when the therapist is inexperienced but of course even with experience it is possible to become over-involved.

Now I knew that it was possible for me to continue working with Susan for three more months but, for reasons that are unnecessary to go into here, I would have to ask her to alter the times of these meetings. So, not only was I going to have to tell her that I would not be fulfilling my original offer of up to two years' contact, but also, should Susan want to see me for the shortened period, she would have to come at a different time. I became convinced that all this would be too much for her to bear and that the best thing to do would be simply to tell her that I was leaving and not offer any more meetings.

Gently, my supervisor put it to me that I seemed unable to allow Susan any say in the matter, that the 'damage' I felt I was going to do by abandoning her was so great that it could not be faced together. Ironically, in my attempt to protect Susan I really was in danger of repeating a pattern she knew so well, and of course it must be asked whom I was really wanting to protect. Surely what I was contemplating had more in common with her first mother, who could only bear to see Susan once, in that I wanted to tell her in a one-off meeting that our contact had to be terminated, rather than allowing her to choose whether she would like to continue seeing me, albeit for only three more months. It is extremely humbling to find that the motives you thought to be primarily connected with your good maternal feelings, can be acted out in a destructive and omnipotent manner.

Chastened but also strengthened by my experience of supervision, I met Susan after the summer break, whereupon she told me that she and her boyfriend were engaged. Having listened to the rest of her news, I said that I wanted to talk to her about our meetings. I told her that I would be leaving in three months' time, that I would be able to continue seeing her up to that date but it would be necessary to ask her to alter the time of our meetings. Susan wept bitterly. When she stopped crying she became silent and withdrawn. I then spoke to her, saying that clearly my decision was very upsetting, and that it must have been confusing to have been seen by one therapist, who could not see her regularly, then be offered appointments with another, who, just as Susan had started to trust her was going to let her down too. It must seem very like what had happened to her in the past. She nodded and began to cry again. I sat bearing Susan's grief but said no more until the end of the session. I told her that we could go on meeting at the arranged time for three more weeks but that after that it would have to be altered. Perhaps she would like to think about what she wanted to do and could let me know when she had decided.

Susan did decide to continue seeing me but did not let me know of her decision until right at the end of the last of her sessions at the original time. Perhaps she needed me to experience how it felt to be left not knowing what was going to happen next but, whatever the reasons, we were able to go on working together. I will not describe the rest of the contact in detail but one or two aspects are relevant. It became clear that it was tremendously important for Susan to feel that I could get on with my own life, unlike her first mother who she felt had ceased living after her birth. She was able to talk about her anger and disappointment with her first mother, and with some of the care she had received from her adoptive mother, and of course from me, the therapist mother. She spoke with some glee about having taken her fiancé home to meet her parents and tell them of her engagement, and discovering that her father, although welcoming, appeared to be a little jealous of this relationship. Throughout these last three months of our contact Susan talked about the possibility of seeing another therapist when I left, since she was entitled to another twenty months of psychotherapy under the rules of practice of the organization. Most of the time she was clear that this was what she wanted but in our last meeting she told me she had changed her mind. Although she might get in touch to take up the possibility of further help, she had decided that she did not want to be offered this automatically. It seemed she preferred to exercise her own control over what happened next, a healthy sign and an understandable decision given what had happened to her when she had no control whatsoever. We parted warmly and with sadness on both sides.

This case demonstrates the importance of a supervisor who can stand outside the therapist/client relationship, and help the supervisee see how her own unconscious feelings may be coming into the work. I was so caught up with my own guilt at abandoning Susan that it seemed to me the best way of managing matters, having made my decision to leave, was to cut myself off quickly and finally. I had rationalized this decision as being in Susan's best interest. Surely it would be better for her not to see me any more once she knew I would be leaving. Clearly, the truth was that it was more to do with my own dread of staying in a relationship to work through the feelings of anger and disappointment with me, the therapist who put herself before her clients. Susan's experience with me had echoes of her past and this fact did not escape her but now she had an opportunity, in the present, to express some of the feelings which had been repressed for so long. She discovered that her adoptive mother could understand her desire to know about the past. And I could become a representation of the mother who abandoned her but could bear to stay with Susan's disappointment and not be damaged by the experience.

SUPERVISION OF STUDENT COUNSELLORS

I will now leave Susan and my own supervision and turn to my role as supervisor. As a tutor on a counselling course I supervise students both at the beginning of their counselling training, as well as at a more advanced level, and the work they are doing is often carried out in settings which make a firm frame extremely difficult to maintain. These difficulties tend to be seen as arising primarily out of the setting and, whilst there is a reality about this, upon closer examination breaks in the frame can often be located in the anxieties which are stirred up in both therapist and client. In training, students are usually eager, excited and enthusiastic, and these attitudes should be encouraged, but eagerness to help and to understand quickly can result in their becoming caught up in the very problems they are trying to help resolve. The teacher who believes in the need for a framework for therapy has to find ways of imparting this belief to students, without becoming persecutory and thus undermining the good-enough work being carried out. All therapists are bound to make mistakes and supervisees need to know that these are accepted by the supervisor before they can begin to discover the importance of regularity, continuity and consistency. Initially, the client's story, the feelings this arouses and the desire to help, are the main focus. It is only gradually and with sensitivity that the supervisor can show how some of the difficulties are located in the way in which issues relating to the frame are being handled. One of the ways I have found of helping counsellors in training, who feel overwhelmed by the problems that are brought to them, is to concentrate on maintaining the framework. To provide a safe and containing environment in which individuals can talk about their difficulties, a place where both the client and the therapist can tolerate not knowing, will lay the foundations for future understanding. The content of sessions needs to be talked about by the counsellor, just as clients need to tell of their life experiences, and the feelings of the supervisee have to be understood by the supervisor. Sensitivity is essential in helping trainees to understand how their interventions may have been experienced by clients, particularly when they arise from feelings of anxiety regarding the frame. When you have gone over a time boundary, lowered a fee, or agreed to take an action, it can feel extremely persecutory to have your supervisor question what you felt to be the only way of managing things. Just as the wise therapist gauges when a particular action falling under the agreed practice should be altered, so supervisors use their judgement in determining when to comment and when not to. The aim of supervision is to protect the primary partnership, the therapist in relationship with client, and to do so the best course is sometimes to let things be. In helping the therapist to maintain a firm framework for the process of therapy, judgement and sensitivity must be the supervisor's main tools.

If you are at the beginning of your career, it is unlikely that you will be able to provide, at first, the sort of framework for therapy I have advocated. It must be abundantly apparent by now, however, that I do not always practise what I preach. Nevertheless, through experience and careful observation, you may start to find that some of the ideas discussed take on a real emotional meaning rather than simply an intellectual one. All therapists from time to time act on the anxieties they experience but if you can begin to understand what is happening, and why it happens with a particular client, you will be in a better position to make considered decisions about the best way to proceed.

THERAPIST AS SUPERVISOR

I am now going to describe my supervision of a student whom I will call Mark. He was on an advanced course and had already got a first qualification but through an organization which was not nationally recognized. The fact that this initial training did not have an academic component was one of the main motivations for Mark seeking further training. In this contact I became increasingly aware that our work together was undermined by Mark's perception of me as persecutory and judgemental. These feelings were accurate, in so far as I did have the power to pass or fail his work, but they also played into anxieties personal to Mark about his competence and his over-valuation of academic qualifications.

The initial contact came not from Mark but through the training organization. I was told that there were difficulties because Mark's current supervisor did not fulfil the institution's criteria for supervision, and that there was disappointment and anger about this, both from supervisor and supervisee. There was also an urgency in finding a new supervisor so that Mark could continue his training. When we met for an initial consultation I suggested to Mark that he talk about one of his cases. He did so and I made several interventions. Mark told me that these were helpful and that he felt he could work with me. I then talked about his previous experience and how difficult it must be to have to change supervisor. It was clear that Mark was angry with the training body for not accepting the person of his choice, but he felt he had to accept this decision because he so wanted the academic qualification. I realized that there was great pressure on Mark to say I was acceptable even if he did not really feel it. He was angry and upset that the supervisor he had worked with for so many years had been rejected and I thought that this must seem like a rejection of his own way of working.

The known and familiar were not acceptable. I suspected that had it not been for Mark's need to have an academic qualification, he would have abandoned the training, but as this need was paramount it overcame his loyalty to the first supervisor. However, it also resulted in a need to please me, the authority figure with a seal of approval from the organization whose approval, was needed by Mark in turn. I did not put this to him, as it seemed to me that these were private concerns, but I was aware they might cause difficulties in the future. Indeed this perception was later to prove accurate. In this first meeting Mark told me that he had been in therapy himself but I had the impression it had not been an altogether helpful experience. When he talked about his practice, which took place in both a private and a public setting, I was impressed by the professionalism and care that was given to his work. We discussed the supervision arrangements, the demands of the course and the requirement of a written report, all of which appeared to be understood and accepted. We agreed to meet weekly.

I quickly found that any questioning on my part seemed to be experienced by Mark as destructively critical, particularly when it came to anything to do with the framework. Lowering a fee, starting a session early, taking telephone calls which went on and on, talking to the partner of a client, altering the times of sessions; all these were seen by Mark as absolute necessities and any understanding of what might lie behind these actions was hard to explore. I was also aware that Mark tended to bring a different case each week and when I suggested that it would be helpful to stay with one client, in order to deepen understanding, whilst this was accepted theoretically, in practice there was always a reason why it was not done. I began to suspect this was a defence and that it stemmed from a fear of revealing to me the anxiety which Mark was experiencing in his contact with clients.

After several months of talking about different cases, Mark told me of a young woman who was causing him particular concern. It was apparent that she had quite extreme difficulties and I suggested it would be helpful to stay with this particular client. The young woman had already had many contacts with social services, all of which she told Mark had been unhelpful. Because the client was unemployed, he had negotiated a fee much lower than his usual charge but now he found that she would often cancel a session or demand a new time. Various reasons were given for this: she had to have her hair done, she had to go shopping, or stay with her boyfriend, who made great demands on her time. Mark appeared to feel guilty about his own critical and angry feelings, particularly regarding the fee, as it was now becoming clear that the client was undervaluing him, in just the way he had undervalued himself in agreeing to a lower charge. When the client was with Mark she would spend much of the time in tears and he found it hard to bring the meetings to a close. To try to make the endings more acceptable, he would give warnings that the time was nearly up but allowed himself to be drawn into conversation when he had indicated that it was time to stop. The client had started telephoning between sessions to ask for advice and help or to tell him that she simply couldn't manage the wait between appointments. Mark told me he had decided she was 'too ill' for him to help her and that she clearly needed to see a psychotherapist rather than a counsellor. I attempted to help Mark see what was going on and how his willingness to accommodate his client, far from being experienced as helpful, was in fact extremely frightening. What he was contemplating doing, ending her contact with him, would be experienced as retaliation for her excessive demands, and indeed it did seem that this was what lay behind his decision. As I spoke I was aware that Mark was unhappy with the way I was understanding what was going on. He seemed to want me to agree with his perception that the client needed the 'expert' help he was unable to provide.

At our next meeting Mark told me that he had not terminated the work with this client but only because I had suggested it would be unhelpful, he still felt she needed to see someone with more expertise. He was extremely angry with me and said he considered this young woman to be at risk and that if she committed suicide, which he thought she might, then I would be responsible. I asked him to tell me about their last meeting and I heard that the young woman had spent the session talking about her mother, her father, and her boyfriend, and how she tried desperately to please them all but to no avail. Whatever she did she always ended up being abandoned. This happened too, she told him, with the social services. They would give her a little help but it was never enough, appointments would be altered, money promised was not forthcoming, and when she complained it was suggested that she should be grateful for what she was getting. Eventually she would be passed on to another department where the whole cycle would start again. 'No one,' she told Mark, 'understands what I need. They judge me and find me wanting.'

I could see that this was what was going to happen with Mark. He was unable to contain the demands of his client and the anxiety she evoked in him would result in him rejecting her, just as everyone else had. I began to say this to Mark but as I did so he suddenly exploded. 'I just cannot work with you, all you ever do is undermine me. You question everything, you are obsessed with money, with nit-picking time-keeping. I've had years of experience and I've been supervised throughout those years and never before have I had anyone question my way of working in the way you do. You obviously think I'm hopeless. I know I'm going to fail and I don't care. I'm going to give this course up, they made me see you, they rejected my supervisor and he thinks the course is rubbish too. It's not worth the paper it's written on.' Mark's anger now turned into tears and he got up to go. I said that I thought it would be better if he stayed so we could talk about what he had just said. 'You seem convinced I don't value what you are trying to do and that the way in which you came to me for supervision has a bearing on this. You also seem convinced I am going to fail you and the fact that I am going to write a report, which does involve passing or failing, seems to have been unhelpful.' More calmly, Mark told me how confused and frightened he had felt by my emphasis on time-keeping, cancellations and fees. It became clear that each time I commented on his work, his anxiety had been such that he was unable to take in what I was saying. The need to be seen as getting everything right had been so great that any questioning was felt by him to mean that nothing was right. Mark also talked of his critical feelings about the tutors on his course and the way it was organized, many of which were quite justified, but all these negative thoughts had been suppressed because of his need to find everything to do with the qualification he so wanted as good and therefore valid.

Now that Mark was able to bring his critical feelings about me and the course into our relationship, he became able to find good in what I had to offer. He began to hear my interventions not as destructively critical but as a way of helping him to contain the feelings of his clients. The anger Mark had felt towards me and which he imagined would result in his failing, now that it had been expressed, enabled him to allow his clients to feel angry with him. He no longer needed to be the perfect therapist, either in terms of having expertise represented in qualifications or in feeling he had to be constantly available. Slowly Mark began to provide a firm framework that allowed his clients to feel and to express those feelings. Of course it was a long and difficult process, particularly with the young woman who had been allowed to contact him at all hours and change her appointments whenever she wanted, but slowly the frame was strengthened, with the result that Mark was less anxious to pass her on to a therapist with better qualifications than his own.

What I learnt from Mark was how closely the supervisory relationship mirrors that of the therapeutic one and how the intrusion of a third party, in the form of a training body, can undermine the learning process. The difficulties of working with Mark, his defensiveness and initially unspoken criticisms of me, stirred up retaliatory feelings, which could have led to me abandoning him, as he wanted to abandon first his client, then his supervision, and finally his training. Because it was so painful to stay in a relationship in which he felt himself to be seen as failure, Mark wanted to fail me. He was identified with both victim and aggressor. Once I had withstood and survived his attack, Mark and I were able to go on to have a relationship founded much more on the realities of the encounter, rather than on phantasies and projections. In fact his angry speech, in which he told me how persecutory I was, came as quite a relief – I felt for the first time that I was allowed to know the real Mark instead of the good supervisee he felt I required him to be. His outburst also enabled me to tell Mark that far from seeing him as a failure, my perception was of a concerned counsellor who worked hard and tried to understand his clients. The fact that he had got so caught up with a particular individual was not evidence of failure, but did need to be understood if Mark was going to be able to continue working with his client – just as I had to understand what had been happening in my relationship with him.

This experience caused me to think hard about the supervisory relationship and what it might mean to students when there is a judgement to be made, a judgement which has to be communicated to a third party, and one that involves passing or failing. There is always the possibility that it will result in supervisees feeling constrained to talk about their work in terms of what they perceive as acceptable to the supervisor. When students write essays to demonstrate their grasp of theory, and how it relates to practice, there are agreed criteria for assessment, as well as procedures for individuals to appeal against what they feel are unfair judgements. When it comes to the supervision of trainees' work with clients, the criteria, although clearly defined, rest on the assessment of one person, the supervisor. We must be aware of the subjectivity this involves. Any breakdown, whether in the therapeutic relationship or the supervisory one, is a shared failure. If counsellors are to be seen as professionals having completed recognized trainings then assessment of students must be part of that training. Supervisors have to contain their own anxieties regarding supervisees' interaction with clients and provide a climate in which learning can take place. If the practical work is deemed unsatisfactory, resulting in a decision to fail the practice, then it is essential that trainees be offered further help so that they can complete their training.

Group supervision has the advantage that individuals often feel more able to challenge the tutor's interpretations when there are fellow students to back them up, but there are disadvantages. The person presenting a case is often overwhelmed by the amount of input, group dynamics can also intrude and the exigencies of time make it difficult to examine case material in depth.

In this chapter I have stressed the importance of supervision, both in terms of the supervisee and the supervisor. If, as I have suggested, the supervisory relationship mirrors the therapeutic one then we might say that it is essential for trainees to have their own experience of therapy. In this way we can understand, in an emotional rather than an intellectual way, what is involved, particularly when it comes to the frame. To know how it feels to long for a session to be extended; to have the fee waived; to become friends with your therapist; to voice these longings and have them understood and contained, will provide the inner strength to contain your clients. To be able to rage against the frame and to find it remains firm, is to have the experience of a form of care that is solid and lasting, a love that embraces hate and does not seek to exclude any emotion, any of the feelings which are a part of all enduring human relationships.

Chapter 11

Ending and evaluation

In this chapter I am going to describe the ending of my work with two clients both of whom have already been discussed – Wendy in Chapters 4 and 7, and Melanie in Chapter 8. I have decided to use these examples for contrast: in one case the work was terminated by the therapist and in the other by the client. I will also discuss how I evaluated the work that was undertaken.

WENDY: THE CLIENT FINDS HER OWN UNDERSTANDING

I will begin with Wendy and remind you that there had already been two interruptions to our work. The first occurred because Wendy decided to take up a placement and the second when she accepted a permanent job, both these decisions making the time of the ongoing appointments impossible. Our last meeting had taken place early in the summer, since when I had come to a decision about my own future, which involved leaving the agency I was working for. This decision had been hard to make and in thinking about what I wanted I was acutely aware of the consequences it might have for the young people I was seeing. I gave a great deal of thought to Wendy and how best to communicate the fact that I would no longer be able to see her on a regular basis. I knew it was right that I should tell her face to face but I found it hard to decide how to initiate this meeting honestly. That is, without raising Wendy's expectations regarding further appointments and yet not imparting the fact of my leaving in a letter. What I decided to write was this:

> Dear Ms Blank,
>
> I know that you are waiting to hear from me regarding further appointments and I think it would be helpful if we could meet to discuss this together.

I am able to see you at 8.00 p.m. on Thursday 23rd September. Please would you let me know whether you are able to come at this time.

Yours sincerely,

Wendy telephoned to confirm this arrangement. When the day came, as she walked into the room I was struck by how relaxed and confident she seemed. And when she sat down I noticed that Wendy had a new hairstyle and was wearing a very smart suit. For a moment it was hard to connect the young woman sitting opposite me with the anxious and rather drab Wendy of our previous meetings. She smiled and asked whether I was now going to see her regularly at this time. I paused for a moment and then responded by saying, 'This is a new time and the one that you told me when we last met would be convenient to you now that you are working.' There was a short pause before Wendy said, 'I don't think you're going to see me regularly at this time because your letter said. . . .' She repeated accurately the precise words I had used. I told Wendy that this was right and that I would be unable to see her again on an ongoing basis because I was leaving the organization at the end of the year. 'Why are you leaving? Where are you going?' Wendy asked. I didn't say anything. 'I expect you're going to do something different,' she said, and then continued to talk almost to herself. 'I don't suppose you're going to tell me why. I do wonder what you're going to do. Perhaps you've got fed up with counselling. Maybe you don't like hearing people go on and on about their problems.'

When she paused, I commented on her feeling that I might not want to keep on hearing about difficulties and where she felt this left her when she still had things she wanted to talk about. Wendy responded by saying that although her problems did not seem as urgent as they had, she still thought she would like to continue with her counselling. She then wondered whether it would be possible for her to see another counsellor, as she knew there was still one year to go of the two years that had been agreed. 'Would it be possible for me to see someone else?' I said that it would. Again she seemed to be having a dialogue with herself. 'I wonder whether I could manage that. It would be difficult. I've got to know you. I do still feel I need help. I wonder what someone else would be like.' Wendy now turned to me, 'What are your colleagues like?' she asked. 'How many of them are there?' I didn't reply. She smiled, 'You won't tell me about the other counsellors. I expect you think it best if I make my own decision about whether to continue. You usually do.' This last comment was made with a broad grin.

Wendy now told me about her job, how she hadn't liked it at first, everyone there was so 'posh', but now she had got used to it and felt fond of her workmates. She felt sure she would stick at it. It was the first time that she had really stuck at anything. I heard about her family and of a row between Wendy, her sister and her mother. It had been sorted out and Wendy had been surprised to discover that she did not feel she had been entirely to blame for the argument. She told me of two young men who were interested in her. She quite liked them but was still not sure she wanted to commit herself to a relationship with someone of the opposite sex. Wendy then came back to the question of counselling and whether she wanted to continue with someone else. 'Would it be possible for me to see a lady therapist? Does it make any difference?' I said that it seemed she felt it might. 'Yes, I feel uneasy with men. One of the psychiatrists I saw was a man but one was a woman and I didn't feel very easy with her either. But you're a woman and I've got used to you. It would be hard to change. Would it be all right for me to ask to see a woman?' I said that she had told me she felt uneasy with men but also with some women too. It did seem hard for her to make her own decision. 'Yes it is. I don't suppose it really makes much difference.' She grappled with the problem before saying firmly, 'Can I see a lady therapist?' I said that I would ask for her to be offered appointments with a woman and checked the times that she would be able to come. Suddenly Wendy's anxieties spilled over in a barrage of questions. 'What happens if I see the person and don't like them? What happens if I don't keep the appointment? Would I be able to ring up and ask to see someone else? Will they think I'm messing them around?' I said it seemed that she felt she wouldn't be forgiven for messing people about and that this was what I had done to her in not keeping to our original agreement. 'Yes, it was hard, I felt shocked when you said you were leaving. I thought it might be because of me.'

Wendy now spoke at length about her father and how terrible she had felt after his death. Just before his suicide she had got into an argument with him and their last words had been angry ones. She told me how depressed he had been, not only immediately before his death but for as long as she could remember. Wendy had felt that her relationship with her father was particularly important to him and that her growing independence had been hard to accept. 'I loved him so much when I was little but as I got older I sometimes hated him for the way he had of making me feel guilty.' For the first time I heard Wendy speak of ambivalence and allow others to have faults rather than seeing herself as the container for all bad feelings. She went on speaking for a long time, making connections between her anxieties and the troubled relationships within the family.

Finally, she came round to the ending of her relationship with me and how much she appreciated the fact that I was telling her face to face that I would be leaving. 'I'm really miles better,' Wendy told me, 'but there are still things I'd like to talk about.' She paused. 'Will you tell your colleagues about me?' she asked. I said, 'You're wondering how private the things are you've told me about. I wonder what you think would be most helpful?' Wendy thought for a moment before replying. 'I used to get so confused. I had such weird ideas in my head. Thinking I'd hurt people. But I don't feel like that any more so I don't suppose there's much point you telling someone about me. I might have changed even more by the time I see them.' There was a long silence before Wendy spoke again, 'I don't know why you're leaving and I don't suppose you'll tell me but I don't think it's because of me.' I smiled and said that it was time for us to say goodbye. Wendy got up, put on her coat, went to open the door and then turned to face me. 'Thank you for all your help. Good luck in whatever you're going to do.'

In this last meeting Wendy is becoming able to make her own decisions and it is clear that her life is beginning to involve relationships with people outside her own immediate family. She is holding down a job and enjoying the contact with her colleagues. Wendy refers to her father and seems to understand that he had difficulties of his own, difficulties that were not solely her responsibility. She also implicity acknowledges the difference between being abandoned, with no opportunity to talk about her feelings, and what was happening in her relationship with me. It felt hard not to give reasons for my leaving, and yet by allowing her to think about this without the reassurance that it was not an escape from her, Wendy was able to find within herself the conviction that it was not she who had made me come to my decision.

One of the areas that gives rise to most criticism in psychotherapy and counselling is that of evaluation. It cannot be based on the subjectivity of either the therapist or the client, as both may have their own conscious and unconscious reasons for seeing the therapy in a particular light. When there is a precise presenting problem, particularly if it is manifested in a physical symptom, then the efficacy of the therapeutic intervention can be evaluated by how far the symptom has been relieved. However, even this is not necessarily evidence for a good outcome, as one symptom can vanish to be replaced by another. Unless taking part in a piece of research with explicit criteria for evaluation, therapists have to rely on something other than their own impressions of what has been achieved. Expressions of gratitude by the client or assurances that the experience has been helpful have to be treated with circumspection. A more objective evaluation is required. I would hasten to add that feelings of gratitude should not be brushed aside – they may be genuine, but they can spring from a need to help the therapist rather than from real changes that have been achieved. It can be extremely hard to tell parents, particularly when you are parting from them, that their care has been anything less than perfect. But most of us know it is the way in which our lives are lived that gives us proof of being enabled or disabled by the care we have received. Children have to separate from their parents to find a way of life that is fulfilling for them, and if we have this in mind we can go some way towards an evaluation of the therapeutic endeavour. We can look for evidence that our clients are overcoming some of the difficulties they have told us of: the relationship with the therapist may be the crucible for change but it is when our clients report improved relationships in the world outside that we begin to know that they are truly helped by their affiliation with us.

In Wendy's case, you may remember that in her first contact with the receptionist she spoke of her worries about the conflict between getting a job and having counselling. She had frightening ideas which were taking her over so that Wendy became more and more isolated. At the point of asking for help a conflict arose regarding the helper. Was this relationship going to result in Wendy being able to achieve an autonomous existence, which would enable her to make other relationships, or would the help make her dependent, keeping her isolated from the world of work that she so much wanted to enter? Another way of thinking about this conflict would be to say that work, for Wendy, equalled adulthood. She needed to experience me as someone who could know about her difficulties and yet also know that I understood her need to be independent of me. Wendy was able to leave me to pursue her desire to work (to be an adult) and this resulted in anxiety, anxiety which I was able to contain by not becoming over-anxious myself. From what she said in our final meeting it seems that Wendy's father may have found it difficult to accept his daughter's growing independence.

Another feature of our contact was the many interruptions caused by Wendy's persistence in pursuing her aim of trying to enter the world of work – of adulthood. The fact that she had to wait before resuming her relationship with me was an important factor in our contact. In these waiting periods, particularly the first, I think Wendy was very uncertain as to what would happen; whether I would really do what I had promised and write when a new time became available. Quite possibly she feared that I would retaliate for her abandonment of me by not wanting to see her again. It was through the experience of finding a secure frame that Wendy was increasingly able to find her own answers to her difficulties. When I came to my decision about leaving the agency, I considered the possibility of postponing my departure date so that I could fulfil what had been agreed with Wendy. I knew as I thought this through that it was unrealistic, and that quite apart from the feelings it might provoke in me, it would place Wendy in the position of the child who cannot face separation. I had to manage my own guilty feelings regarding abandonment and broken promises, and not avoid them. Wendy helped me to recognize how vitally important it is for therapists to think carefully about the words they use. She also helped me to be honest about partings, and not to avoid the reality of leaving someone by taking refuge in rationalization or reassurance. By the time we parted Wendy still had problems, but there was firm evidence that in going out to work and leaving what had become the isolation of her home, she was moving towards an autonomous and fulfilling life.

MELANIE: GIVING UP THE SEARCH FOR PERFECTION

Autonomy was also an issue in my work with Melanie. You will remember that I had become identified and sympathetic rather than objective and empathic, an over-involvement resulting in breaks in the frame, which had to be remedied before the therapeutic environment could be experienced as enabling rather than disabling. When the fee that had been agreed in the initial consultation was reinstated, Melanie became more able to bring her doubts about me and our relationship into the sessions. The idealization on both sides began to break down: Melanie was able to see me as less than perfect and I was able to see her as an ordinary human being grappling with day-to-day difficulties. One of the ways in which Melanie brought her negative feelings about me into our work was through her resentment at having to pay for something she felt should have been hers as of right. The original fee had been restored but now she talked of financial hardships and how psychotherapy ought to be available free of charge.

One day she told me that she was going to see her doctor to find out whether psychological help could be provided through the National Health Service. I was assured that her relationship with me was important and that Melanie appreciated I had to charge for my services, but perhaps her GP would find a way of her coming to see me which did not mean she had to pay for the time herself. I knew that I could interpret these feelings in terms of her longing to have what she felt had been denied her in childhood, unconditional love, but I felt that although this might have been accepted intellectually, it was important for Melanie to be able to experience her disappointment and anger more directly. She told me that she had been referred by her GP to a psychiatrist for an assessment. Melanie was excited by the prospect and of the possibility of having what she wanted without having to pay for it.

In these communications I felt myself under extreme pressure in having to contain what were implicit criticisms of me, and of course, in the event of Melanie being offered free therapeutic help, the ending of our relationship. I found myself wanting to give her the 'benefit' of my own knowledge of the difficulties of obtaining psychotherapy through the auspices of the NHS, and that it was extremely unlikely money would be provided to pay a private therapist. But when I thought about any reasons for wanting to do this I was aware of complex feelings: I wanted to save Melanie from what I suspected would be disappointment and, because it felt like a retaliation for what I was not providing – unconditional love – I wanted her to know that no one else could give her what she felt I refused. When I analysed my own ambivalent feelings, I decided that the best course was to accept Melanie's ambivalence, let her explore the alternatives for herself and simply to wait and see what would happen next.

I was not allowed to know the outcome of the meeting between Melanie and the psychiatrist until several weeks after it had occurred, and I suspect that this was because the disappointment and anger had been so overwhelming. Apparently Melanie had been told that the likelihood of help through the NHS was remote. She could go on a waiting list but would not be seen for well over a year. When she told me this, Melanie railed against the system that was so unresponsive to her needs. I understood this as a representation of the rage she felt towards me, the therapist who demanded payment in return for care. To interpret along these lines might well have been accurate, in a theoretical sense, but it seemed to me that to speak in these terms might be experienced by Melanie as correct and yet sterile. What I decided would be more helpful would be to withstand the barrage of complaints and criticisms, knowing them to be directed at me, yet without delivering the rather obvious interpretation. This I thought would allow Melanie to experience me as able to contain the onslaught without taking refuge in words: the interpretation that I composed in my mind was rejected because it felt as if my words were an escape from experience into the realm of intellect.

In the following months our work together continued and increasingly I was allowed to know of Melanie's doubts about her own ability as a mother, and of her longing for another child. It might be that as I relinquished my role as the ideal therapist, Melanie allowed me to know that she too was less than perfect. When she talked about the possibility of another baby, I was aware of my own concern for Melanie and what might happen if a second child was born with the same disability, a real possibility. This time, however, I was alert to the difficulties associated with the concept of perfection and how it pervaded our relationship. The question of the cost of therapy still came up, not in requests for a lower fee but through conflicting needs in Melanie. On the one hand there was her desire to have a second baby with all the costs this would involve, and on the other there was her wish to keep on seeing me, at a price.

Gradually Melanie worked through some of her dilemmas: first she decided she definitely wanted to become pregnant, and then she thought about having another child who just might, like Sally, be born with a handicap. After talking to her husband they both agreed that in the event of pregnancy Melanie should not have amniocentesis; they would welcome another baby whatever imperfections it might have. She continued to be uncertain of whether her relationship with me was one that should go on or whether she could manage on her own, knowing she could have free psychotherapy in the future. Finally she decided that she did still need my help, and that if she became pregnant she would take a break for the birth and then come back. But she also began to talk about the support she was increasingly able to get from her own mother. Friends, who hitherto had been thought to be too preoccupied with their own concerns, offered help with the care of Sally. Her husband assured Melanie that despite financial difficulties there was enough money to pay for her to keep on seeing me. Then the longed-for event happened – Melanie was pregnant. She reported with evident delight how she had seen the consultant who had attended Sally's birth, and had been able to tell him of the shortcomings in the way that she was treated subsequently – another example, I thought, of an unconscious communication of how she had experienced the shortcomings in the care I had provided.

Three months later Melanie said that she was thinking of stopping her sessions. She had deliberated a lot she said and had considered ending on that day, because the idea of telling me and then carrying on seemed impossible. Upon reflection she had decided not to do this, but it felt very strange and difficult. As she talked it became evident that Melanie was worried about me and my feelings. Would I be hurt? Would I think it was because I had not been perfect? By now of course I knew I had not been and had ceased trying to be! In the last two months of our meetings Melanie was able to go on thinking and talking about perfection, about what impossible goals she had to set herself and others, and about her disappointment with those who let her down. That I was one of those people was clear, but the fact that we had managed to stay in a relationship, and that errors had been worked through and forgiven, helped Melanie to find good in herself and in her family and friends. In our final meeting Melanie told me that she had received a letter offering her psychotherapy on the NHS. But now she said she had decided not to accept the offer.

Like all the people I have described, Melanie's difficulties were not entirely resolved. Doubtless she would continue to expect much of herself and be disappointed when she failed to reach her own high standards, but there was evidence that her situation had improved. Her capacity to be a mother had not been undermined by the experience of having a child who was less than perfect, and her own experience of being mothered was no longer seen in entirely negative terms. Melanie became increasingly able to see her own mother as a provider of help and support. Her courage in deciding not to have a test to determine whether or not her unborn baby had any defects was extremely moving. Melanie was not anti-abortion on principle, believing it to be up to individuals to make their own decisions, but with her husband she thought long and deeply about what they would do if the test indicated a less than perfect foetus. Melanie and he both knew that they had the capacity to love their unborn child whatever sort of person he or she turned out to be. It was a moving testimony to the power of human love and a triumph not so much over adversity but through adversity.

Before I end this chapter there is something I want to say about therapeutic work in general, which also has connections with evaluation. It concerns anxiety. It seems to me that one of the primary tasks for the therapist is to contain anxiety, and it is this containment which is essential before the next step of understanding can be achieved. There is often a tendency to speak to the anxiety, as it were, before the therapist has any idea of what it stems from. Difficult as it is, the therapist must be able to stay with anxiety and let it develop before attempting to interpret. This can feel cruel and uncomfortable, but to avoid this unpleasant feeling is rather like a doctor deciding not to examine a suppurating wound because it might cause the patient pain. Instead a sedative is given, both doctor and patient feel better, the doctor avoids causing more pain and the patient's distress is temporarily relieved, but the reasons for the wound remain unknown. Rather like the doctor who decides that sore places need further investigation, the therapist does not avoid anxiety but seeks to understand it, knowing that this will take time and that it may be necessary for both client and therapist to experience discomfort in the process.

Freud's delightful description of his grandson's game with a wooden reel and a piece of string pointed the way to his understanding of how children master anxiety. I have found this useful to have in mind as one of the aims of the therapeutic relationship. The one-and-a-half-year-old in Freud's example was very attached to his mother and yet surprisingly never protested when she left him. Freud observed the little boy's play: a wooden reel attached to a long piece of string was thrown into a curtained crib so that it disappeared. The child uttered a sound which corresponded to the German word for 'gone'. He then pulled the string until the reel reappeared, when it was met with a delighted cry of 'da' (there). Freud understood this game in terms of the child mastering the anxiety he felt when his mother left him, being able in the play to control both the disappearance and reappearance of the object. Freud goes on to remind us of the importance of mastering anxiety: 'the child's great cultural achievement – the instinctual renunciation (that is, the renunciation of instinctual satisfaction) which he made in allowing his mother to go away without protesting' (Freud, 1984: 285).

We can learn from this what the mother in Freud's example did intuitively, that is, she allowed her child to experience and overcome anxiety. Perhaps this is what we as therapists must do. We must not become over-anxious ourselves and seek to allay or reassure but provide a safe-enough environment in which anxiety can be experienced. This idea can also be applied to evaluation so that we do not try to see the work we have undertaken simply in terms of success or failure. We might instead look for evidence of how far we have enabled our clients to experience anxieties, understand and overcome them. In those areas where this has not been achieved we do not have to castigate ourselves, but it may be possible to think about why particular aspects of the work have proved to be so difficult and how they relate to our own unresolved anxieties.

The framework for therapy provided by the therapist is like the holding the mother offers her child but it is not the same. Parents actively seek to comfort, reassure and alleviate infant anxieties and that this is never wholly successful is inevitable. The child is not simply a passive entity, and also plays a part in mastering frightening experiences. Through the interplay of emotions, parent and child sometimes succeed and at other times fail in this task. In some instances anxiety is mastered but in others the anxiety remains, only to surface again, often in situations that do not at first appear to have any connection with the original source. The frame could be seen as both the source and the potential container for the re-enactment of anxieties that have been experienced in the past. As artists create their pictures, so anxieties will surface and play their part in the creative process. When the picture is complete the artist has mastered the very anxieties that motivated the need to create – or, it might be truer to say, partially mastered, for surely the dissatisfaction that is also experienced when an important piece of work is ended is evidence that it is never perfect. Some anxieties remain. When we observe the artist's creation we may ourselves be conscious of the great achievement, 'the renunciation of instinctual satisfaction', and some of the satisfaction we derive is through an unconscious recognition and identification with the anxieties that have been struggled with and overcome.

Similar feelings are experienced in the theatre where the stage becomes the container for the anxieties the players are to act out and eventually master. We might imagine that all creative activity, whether it is the child at play or the artist at work, requires some concept of containment. For the child perhaps it is a time boundary, the knowledge that play will end when it is teatime or bedtime. The forces of reality impose their own demands. But in play itself children demonstrate their need for containment in that their playful activities are often excessively rule-bound. Woe betide the child who does not conform to the agreed practice for a particular game. For artists, too, prosaic needs for food and sleep intrude on the creative process. They also need their 'play' to be contained – in the covers of a book, the frame for a canvas, or the stage for a performance. Unless this is provided, the work is chaotic, and we might say that the disturbed feelings provoked by lack of containment stem from a recognition that anxiety has not been overcome – it spills out all over the place. Of course there are times when this is deliberate: the play in which a member of the audience finds the person sitting next to her is in fact an actor and the speech he makes not the outpourings of a madman but part of the performance, is disturbing and confuses the boundaries between reality and fantasy.

The therapeutic frame is like the artist's frame and like the framework for care provided by parents for their children. It is something that both initiates and curtails the interaction of the two people contained within – it is both a source of anxiety and a container for anxiety. Without a framework neither participant in the therapeutic relationship will feel safe enough to experience the complex emotions that are part of all deep and lasting relationships.

Afterword

What I have written is primarily intended for therapists at the beginning of their training and therefore the examples of casework I have used concern individuals seen on a once-weekly basis. This was a deliberate decision, because I wanted to show that it is possible to address problems, sometimes of a quite severe nature, even when the contact is relatively infrequent, and in some cases time-limited. When clients are seen three, four or five times weekly over a long period of time, the therapeutic relationship is not intrinsically different and the frame is just as important. But the process will involve skills of communication that have only been touched on in this book. My own experience of becoming a therapist leads me to think that it may be an important part of development to learn to be silent before we can take the next step of learning how to speak to our clients. When we are inexperienced we often feel a pressure to understand quickly which results in too much talk on our part. Maintaining the frame is an extremely difficult task in itself and if this can be seen as a central concern the therapist will be experienced as containing. Thus the pressure to understand the content of all that the client is communicating may feel less great. By allowing ourselves not to know, our attention is able to be more free-floating – the state of mind necessary to understand the unconscious elements in communication. We no longer get caught up in the manifest or surface content and can recognize themes not apparent to the client. Connections can be made and therapists may recognize, in the stories they are told, how they are being perceived by the client. To see someone four or five times weekly over many years requires us to be in touch with primitive emotions, feelings that are beyond words for the client but which need to be understood and articulated by the therapist. Before we can move into this realm, we need to learn how to provide a framework that makes it possible for both therapist and client to work at this depth.

All of us go on developing for better or for worse both in our personal and professional lives. The ways of working I have advocated and described were developed at one stage in my work as a therapist, and now as I come to the end of this book I am at a different stage. I am already conscious of changes of emphasis, new ways of approaching and understanding the framework for therapy, as well as the omissions I have made because of the concentration on a particular way of thinking. However, there comes a time when it is necessary to let matters stand, for good or ill – that is how you were, this is what you thought. It may be that with the passage of time we look back and wish we could change aspects of the past, but this is not possible. We can only alter our way of looking at things from our vantage point in the present. This painful fact has to be faced, and is faced over and over again in the therapeutic relationship. Our history has to stand but it does not have to dominate our future. We may not be able to alter the facts of our past but we can come to terms with them. We can forgive ourselves and others, let bygones be bygones, and get on with living our lives.

Throughout this book I have understood the therapeutic relationship in terms of parents and children but this understanding is an internal concept, rather than one that is spoken. All families have their own rules of conduct, which develop out of their own individual experiences within their own particular culture. We must respect differences, try to understand them, and not impose our own ideas unthinkingly. I have advocated firm rules for practice but suggested that actions falling under those rules be considered case by case. We may find the failure to apply a rule is ultimately unhelpful; indeed this is often so, but it need not be disastrous. When we have discovered what a break in the frame means to a particular client, we can use this knowledge to inform our practice when we are faced with similar situations. Each person we see teaches us about the therapeutic process, and as we gain more and more experience we build up a set of general rules, which are applied until a particular case makes us rethink our practice. In most instances we will find that breaking a rule is unhelpful, but it may be necessary for it to happen before we can be sure. People have to know that we are primarily concerned with them as individuals, not with an abstract set of rules imposed in an arbitrary fashion. This applies not only to the frame but to everything we say to the people we see. Textbook interpretations or stereotyped responses leave individual difficulties untouched. The clumsiest of comments, springing from a real attempt to address the person with you in your consulting room, will be far more effective than a clever interpretation – however theoretically accurate it may be.

Glossary of terms

As well as the terms used in the text there are also some additions: concepts that are closely connected with the one under discussion, or new terms which simply provide further clarification of the ideas discussed in the book. Because one of my aims has been to simplify theoretical terminology, I have included practical examples of how some of the concepts might inform therapeutic work.

Acting out   Actions that stem from unconscious wishes. In the therapeutic setting the transference will activate feelings that have been subject to repression. It is these that may be acted out – literally, in the world outside the consulting room, in a new relationship, for example. In this situation feelings are stirred up, through the transference, and unless and until they are understood, they will continue to be acted upon. We do not necessarily have to see acting out as 'wrong'. Indeed relationships formed outside the therapeutic setting may be influenced by the therapy in a positive way. However, it is helpful to have this concept in mind, particularly when acting out appears to be an avoidance of feelings that need to be understood within the context of the therapy. We must remember, too, that although this term is usually used in connection with the client, it is also possible for therapists to act out. Whenever we become aware of wanting to take an action we should try to understand what is motivating us – are we acting out something that really belongs to the client or to unresolved difficulties of our own? It is also possible for 'acting in' to occur. This refers again to unconscious wishes, but this time, rather than actions occurring outside the therapy, they are acted on within the treatment setting.

Ambivalence   The co-existence of contradictory feelings, particularly those of love and hate. All of us have difficulty with ambivalence, tending to split off whichever emotion interferes with our desired perception. In the therapy setting we need to be aware of what is split off, as one of our aims will be to further the tolerance of ambivalence.

Attachment   Term used to denote the way infants bond with their mothers. John Bowlby's work helped us to understand the way in which young animals and young humans evoke care from their parents. In his book *The Making and Breaking of Affectional Bonds* (Bowlby 1979) he describes the way in which attachments are made and the distress that results when these bonds are broken.

Congruence   Quality of being congruent: of there being agreement between things. This is a quality that is stressed in person-centred counselling, and it can raise problems for the therapist. If we are to be congruent – to allow a connection between what we feel and how we respond – what are we to do with, say, dislike or fear when we experience these emotions towards our clients? This is where an understanding of the countertransference can help, and points the way to how these feelings can be used therapeutically. First of all we can acknowledge to ourselves what we feel. By making conscious emotions that seem anti-therapeutic, we are able to take the next step, that of thinking. This will lead us on to an understanding of why the client arouses such difficult feelings (something that the client probably knows already), which may be a defence to prevent intimacy. It is when we deny what we feel that we will be incongruent. It is not necessary to give voice to our feelings.

Countertransference   Therapists' feelings and reactions to their clients. Initially, countertransference was given little attention because these feelings were seen as interfering with what was essentially 'treatment', in the sense of a doctor treating a patient. In other words, the therapist was seen as neutral and her/his feelings were not considered to be relevant. However, as it became increasingly understood that it was the therapeutic relationship itself that was curative, not just the therapist's interpretations, so the concept of countertransference became increasingly important. It is still the subject of debate and controversy.

Defences   The mechanisms we all employ to prevent particular feelings gaining expression. In the therapeutic setting we should be alert to these mechanisms and how they are operating, both in ourselves and in our clients. Whatever is felt to be unacceptable or unbearable will be defended against. For instance, through denigration we may be defending against loving feelings, or by idealization we may avoid feelings of hate. Defences are extremely useful: they help us to avoid situations which provoke unbearable anxieties. But of course they can also prevent us from living life to the full. In therapy we often discover that some of our defensive manoeuvres can be abandoned.

Depressive position   A term used by Melanie Klein to indicate a position reached by infants when they are able to perceive their mothers as whole objects. Prior to this, good and bad are kept separate, so that mother is either all good or all bad – the paranoid/schizoid state. Reaching the depressive position involves knowing that one person can be the source of both good and bad feelings – holding ambivalence. All of us revert to the paranoid/schizoid state at times, and the depressive position will also be reactivated throughout our lives. We might hope that at the ending of therapy our clients will experience feelings associated with the depressive position, so that we are neither idealized nor denigrated but seen as both helpful and, at times, unhelpful.

Ego   In a topographical sense, that part of our mind concerned with mediating between the demands of external reality and the imperatives of the id. The ego is the thinking or conscious part of our mind. In Latin 'ego' means 'I', and this sense of ourselves as separate and distinct from anyone else is at first weak. We might think of a newborn infant as having no ego, no concept of itself as separate from mother. Ego-strength is developed through the mother or mother substitute gradually introducing 'reality' – allowing the environment to impinge on the child. In this way the infant is increasingly able to tolerate frustration. It is useful for therapists to bear in mind the need to develop ego-strength, and to remember the urgency of the desire for instant gratification.

Empathy   Power of entering into another's personality and imaginatively experiencing her/his experience. This is a concept that is emphasized in person-centred counselling but of course it is important in all forms of therapy. Particularly at the beginning of our careers we often confuse empathy with sympathy, and with identification. One of the definitions of sympathy is to enter into another's mind with harmonious understanding. The distinction between empathy and sympathy lies in the word 'imaginatively'. We do not respond as if we know exactly how our clients feel – sympathy; we imagine how things feel to them – empathy. Similarly, when we identify with someone we feel their experiences as our own, which will inhibit empathy. Therapists need to be empathic but, in not offering sympathy or becoming identified with their clients, they retain objectivity and separateness. This allows us to think about our clients rather than becoming overwhelmed by them, or over-involved with them.

Flight into health   See below.

Flight into illness   A figurative expression to describe what happens when we look to illness as way of escaping psychic conflict. For instance, it may be that we develop a headache rather than face the conflict of dealing with a particularly difficult situation at work. The headache is real but the result of the illness is an escape from conflict – a gain. This is a very simple example, but of course much more serious illnesses can result from psychic conflicts. By extension, flight into health may also provide a means of escape. In the therapeutic context we may wonder whether physical symptoms are masking psychic conflicts and, should a client suddenly announce that all his or her problems are solved, we might consider the possibility of this being flight into health. An appreciation of both these concepts can inform the therapist's understanding.

Free association   Giving voice to whatever thoughts come to mind, no matter how apparently random and meaningless. By allowing one thought to follow freely from another, the trained listener can connect and understand unconscious elements in the communication. This is because the unconscious always associates one idea with another, even if the association is hidden from the speaker. Should free association cease the therapist is alerted to resistances. Some practitioners suggest that this method is advocated, in the sense of actually telling the client to free associate, but this in itself may be very frightening, particularly in the early stages of therapy. However, even if at first the client has to be 'helped' to speak, it is useful to remember that what we are aiming for is a situation in which people can put words to whatever thoughts and ideas come into their minds. We should also remember that what often prevents free association is the presence of the therapist, and by understanding who we may represent, in the transference, we may help our clients to speak more freely.

Good-enough   Term coined by D.W. Winnicott to convey the idea of the sort of care that most mothers provide for their children: not perfect, and not entirely deficient, but good-enough. It is now used more widely to describe all human endeavours.

Id   In a topographical sense, that part of the mind which contains all our instinctual impulses – the forces driving our actions which are essentially unknown. It can be equated with the unconscious. The demands of the id clamour for attention, particularly in infancy, but increasingly the ego is able to mediate between instinctual needs and the forces of reality. At first the mother acts for her infant: we could see her as performing the functions of the as yet undeveloped infant ego. Initially she responds very quickly to demands for attention – the id is imperious. But, by allowing longer and longer periods of time to elapse between feeds, say, she is able to let the infant's developing ego take over the task of coping with frustration. Again, this idea can inform our work as therapists: through our ability to contain rather than act, and to communicate our understanding of how our clients feel, we help them to tolerate frustration. Unlike the mother, we do not take over the functions of the ego, but we do try to appreciate the demands of the id.

Idealization Device that most of us employ to elevate qualities either in ourselves or in others to a point of perfection. We need to be aware of this tendency because, in the therapeutic setting, it may be used to avoid opposing feelings. We should remember that the other side of this particular coin is denigration. Idealization cannot be sustained forever and when it disintegrates we may be left with despair, which in turn will lead to denigration. Clients who leave therapy with an idealized image take away with them not a real representation of care that is good-enough but a fragile and false image that will inevitably collapse.

Identification The way in which we assimilate attributes of an other into our own personality. We go on identifying throughout life, but it is particulary in infancy and childhood that this process operates, as it is through identifications that we become who we are. There are two ways of thinking about this concept in the therapeutic setting. The first is a positive sense: we may provide a model for identification – people who can both care for our clients and care for ourselves. In other words, clients can identify or assimilate those attributes that will enable them to experience the therapist as both connected to them, and yet separate from them. In this way the identification with the therapist allows the client to remain autonomous. The second sense is a negative one and occurs when the client identifies with the therapist 'as if' they were one. In this case the client may feel that the only way of living is to be what others are, or expect them to be, a situation that will inevitably lead to enormous frustrations, denial of separateness and loss of selfhood.

Internalization Process whereby we take into ourselves attributes, qualities, ideas or situations. For instance, in childhood we may have internalized a sense of being important through the care we have received from our parents. Or, we may have internalized a prohibition – it is always wrong to steal. Something that has originally been outside is taken in and becomes part of ourselves. These internalizations are so bound up with our sense of self that it is often hard to appreciate that once we did not have this feeling, or that idea. In therapy it can be quite liberating for people to discover that some internalizations are not absolutes but simply belong to past experiences that can, if they wish, be discarded.

Interpretation   Procedure which brings out the latent or unconscious meaning underlying the manifest communication. An interpretation will connect the unconscious wish both with the past (the original object of the wish) and with the present (the client's relationships in the external world) and with the person of the therapist. Interpretation is not always given such a precise meaning: it is often used to describe any comment the therapist makes which seeks to 'explain' the client's present situation, whether in their relationships with people outside the therapeutic setting or with the therapist.

Latency period   Phase of development when infantile sexuality undergoes repression, beginning around the age of five and continuing until the onset of puberty.

Nursing triad   Metaphor used by Patrick Casement to describe the need for three people to be involved in the first few months of an infant's life. During this phase, when the mother is intensely preoccupied with the baby, she needs someone to provide support and emotional holding, so that all her attention can be directed towards the infant. This function is usually performed by the biological father, or, if he is absent, by any adult who can protect the primary partnership (Casement, 1985). Casement also uses the metaphor of the nursing triad to emphasize the need for a supervisor to 'hold' the therapist, particularly in the training phase. The anxieties stirred up in therapists in their relationships with clients can be acute and, if they are not contained, can lead to various forms of acting out which may endanger the therapy. The supervisor performs a similar function to the person who supports the mother in her involvement with her child, thus protecting and helping maintain the primary relationship.

Object   The aim of an instinctual drive. The word 'object' does not only refer to inanimate things but also to people. An easy way to help us think about this term is to remember that we often say: 'The object of our desire is. . . .' In the therapeutic setting, the therapist will often come to represent the original objects of desire – parents – and understanding how important we are to our clients helps us to be sensitive in all that we say or do.

Oedipus complex This refers to a constellation of feelings children experience towards their parents – very simply, hostile thoughts towards the parent of the same sex and loving feelings towards the parent of the opposite sex. Freud believed that the Oedipus complex, and its resolution, played a fundamental part in the structuring of personality. Oedipal feelings emerge, according to Freud, first in early childhood, then during the latency period they are subject to repression, only to emerge again in adolescence. Different psychoanalytic schools of thought place differing emphases on oedipal feelings, when they first occur, how they influence later development and how fundamental they are. It is well worth reading a good account of the original Greek myth, as well as Sophocles' *Oedipus Rex*, before tackling psychoanalytic explanations. This is because the Oedipus complex has been trivialized, not through Freud's interpretation but because we all tend to think we know what the story involves and what Freud thought. It is also important to look at other ways of interpreting human development, since not all theories see the oedipal triangle as central to understanding.

Omnipotence Unlimited power – a state believed to be experienced in infancy. This concept was developed from Melanie Klein's work with young children, and from observations of infants. The theory is that when the infant is responded to, this response will be experienced as being created out of itself – thus as omnipotence. In other words, say a baby feels the sensations of hunger and as it does so the breast is offered, then the baby will feel it has created the breast. Alternatively, should a child feel angry with a parent and have hostile feelings, then if the parent becomes ill, the child may experience thoughts as synonymous with deeds – thus as omnipotence. Feelings of omnipotence are a defence against the reality of being small and powerless and it is an important part of development that they are given up. Therapists need to be alert to omnipotent phantasies, either in connection with their own healing powers, or in connection with feelings their clients have towards them. Although as adults we know that thoughts are not actions, we can still feel very guilty when we have spoken or thought badly of someone who then becomes unwell. Clients can become excessively worried about their therapists and, particularly in the case of clients who tend to idealize, we may wonder whether this anxiety could be the result of aggressive or hostile feelings, feelings that are too dangerous to express openly.

Pleasure principle One of the two principles which, according to Freud, govern mental life. Freud believed that psychic activity was aimed at avoiding unpleasure and procuring pleasure. For further discussion see **Reality principle**.

Projection Operation whereby we expel feelings, qualities or wishes so that they are relocated in another person. We may be projecting when we criticize someone for their narrow-mindedness, rather than admitting to a narrow outlook ourselves. Or, we may see in a friend all those qualities we long to have, failing to recognize that we too have positive aspects to our personality. In both cases we are projecting parts of ourselves and seeing them in another. Projection is such a universal phenomenon that it is almost bound to come into the therapeutic setting. It is a particularly useful concept for helping us to recognize and understand those parts of our clients that they find unacceptable.

Projective identification Mechanism closely associated with the paranoid-schizoid position, when split-off parts of the self are projected in order to control or injure. It is a mode of projection. The term 'identification' is added because it is the subject's self that is projected rather than a quality or attribute. When we become the recipient of a projective identification, we may be unaware of the projection and act as if the feelings were our own, that is, we are controlled by the object. Sometimes it is possible, when we can understand what is happening, to speak to the projection rather than act on it. For example, we might find ourselves extremely frightened by a client, but if we are able to think about what is happening this can help us to contain the projection. It may be that feelings have to be put into therapists so that they can experience, in this direct way, how it feels to be the client. By containing rather than acting, and finding words to speak to the feelings, we can help the client take back their projection.

Reality principle One of the two principles which, according to Freud, govern mental functioning. It is coupled with and modifies the pleasure principle. The reality principle is essentially regulatory and delays the gratification of instinctual wishes. It is concerned with external realities – parental prohibitions, consequences stemming from actions, disapproval, and so on. The pleasure principle is concerned with what is internal – instinctual wishes craving satisfaction. At first, it is argued, pleasure is our only aim, but gradually the infant learns that instant gratification is not always possible – the reality principle. In the therapeutic setting, the therapist can become the object of the client's need for gratification but the forces of reality impose restraints on how far these can be met. It is important to be aware of the frustrations that are experienced by the demands of the reality principle.

Regression   To return to a former point or state – in the therapeutic setting, a return to past phases of development. Through the feelings evoked by the transference the client becomes regressed, so that feelings belonging to infancy and childhood can be re-experienced in the immediacy of the relationship with the therapist.

Reparation   Restoring to a proper state. A mechanism described by Melanie Klein, whereby the object is felt to be damaged by destructive phantasies located in the subject, which then lead to a need to make good. When we feel we have damaged someone, particularly someone we love, we also experience anxiety and guilt. The concept of reparation is an important one in therapy. Our clients may have many destructive thoughts and phantasies and we should appreciate their need to make good the damage – real or imagined. This is why, in the therapeutic setting, it is best not to reassure. For instance, clients might fear that they have hurt us through something they have said or done. By containing our need to reassure we may open up the possibility for aggressive thoughts to be brought into the open. In so doing our clients discover that all their feelings are accepted, not just the 'good' ones. When we are able to trust the therapist enough to speak of our hostile and aggressive impulses, and find that these feelings are accepted and understood, this itself can be experienced as reparation – things are restored to a proper state. The concept of reparation is closely associated with the depressive position.

Repression   Occurs when we confine to the unconscious, thoughts, memories or ideas that are bound to an instinct, an instinct that although pleasurable in itself would incur displeasure – because of a prohibition. A common misunderstanding of Freud's ideas is to see repression as 'bad', to think that in order to be happy we have to be free from the guilt associated with repression. Rather, one of our aims as therapists might be to understand why certain thoughts or feelings have been repressed – to make conscious the unconscious – and in so doing to enable our clients to make choices, rather than remaining in the grip of the unconscious. Repression is necessary because it prevents us from experiencing the constant demands of the id.

Resistance   Anything that obstructs us from gaining access to what is unconscious. We often find that individuals entering therapy, at first seem to have no difficulty in talking about their problems, and indeed often seem to be responding well to our interventions – the honeymoon period. This phase is usually shortlived, and when it ends we need to be aware of resistance. We try to understand what is preventing the free flow of thoughts.

Separation anxiety   Refers originally to the anxieties experienced by an infant separated from its mother – a potentially life-threatening situation. This anxiety may be experienced in other situations involving separation. In the therapeutic setting clients may feel anxious about separating from the therapist, whether at the end of a session, when there are vacation breaks, or when the therapy comes to an end.

Splitting   A defence that allows us to keep separate what are really two sides of the same coin. It is a mechanism that we see in operation all the time: good/bad, black/white, god/devil, male/female, etc. When our clients speak in terms of absolute divisions we should be alerted to the defensive mechanism of splitting.

Super-ego   The third agency of the personality, the other two being the ego and the id. An easy way to think about the super-ego is to equate it with conscience – the part of our mind that often prohibits us from doing what we want to do. Freud suggested that through the dissolution of the Oedipus complex the super-ego was formed, because parental prohibitions were internalized. There is debate regarding precisely at what age this occurs. As well as parental prohibitions, we take into ourselves judgements, rules, notions of right and wrong, whether advocated by individuals or by the strictures of the society we inhabit. Therapists need to be aware of the possibility of an over-harsh super-ego, and part of their task may be to help the clients form their own moral codes, rather than holding on to the strictures which have been rigidly internalized from others.

Transference   The re-emergence of infantile prototypes which, in the therapeutic setting, are transferred on to the therapist. In psycho-analytically oriented therapies, it is through the transference that problems are played out, and the resolution of the transference defines the cure. What is meant by 'cure' is that projections are slowly withdrawn, so that therapists are no longer seen predominantly as parental figures but become what of course they always were, ordinary people with a particular expertise, and the transference is resolved. Analytic therapy often takes place over a number of years. This is because the therapeutic relationship becomes what we might term an 'as if' one. In other words, therapists will often be responded to in sessions as if they were parents. The frequency of the meetings, and the fact that they take place over a long period of time, allows for regression. In this way, through the intensity of the encounter, very early feelings of dependency can slowly be worked through. Of course transference feelings are present in all therapies, including short contacts. Time-limited and less frequent meetings, however, do not usually provide the sort of containment necessary for deep regression. And of course many people can neither afford a long course of treatment, nor do they necessarily want intensive therapy. The way in which the transference is understood and used, or not used, depends both on the theoretical school we follow and on the sort of people we are.

Transitional object   A term given by D.W. Winnicott to the comforters that little children use – a favourite toy or a piece of blanket. They represent something that is both mother and not mother, and can be used to express all sorts of feelings: love, hate, aggression, reparation, etc. The important thing is that these loved possessions are able to survive all the feelings children have towards them. They are termed transitional because they help in the move from the original object, the mother, towards a more independent state.

Unconditional positive regard   A therapeutic stance advocated in person-centred counselling. This causes much debate amongst trainees, as it is often taken to mean 'liking' or 'approving'. The way I understand what is intended by the term is not that therapists have to like their clients all the time, or that they should approve of all their actions, but that the therapeutic attitude is one of acceptance. Clients are understood within their own frames of reference – through empathy – not from any external moral code, whether it is society's or the therapist's own. A belief in the integrity of the individual and a respect for all people, no matter how different their experiences are from our own, is fundamental. This does not mean that we will never be shocked by what we are told, nor does it mean that we are 'not allowed' to experience feelings of dislike or disapproval – to deny these emotions would result in the therapist being incongruent – we simply accept what we feel, just as we accept what the client feels. In time, as we gain more and more understanding of the particular client, so we discover that our 'negative' feelings drop away. We are not concerned with judging, approving or condoning, but with accepting. Unconditional positive regard, as I understand it, is an attitude adopted by the therapist, an attitude of acceptance which embraces every aspect of the client's personality.

Unconscious   All those thoughts and feelings that are outside awareness. Freud of course did not discover the unconscious, which has always been there, but he described and defined the way in which our actions can be driven by wishes that are concealed from conscious thought. These hidden motives are revealed in dreams, and through the associations that can be discovered in apparently random utterances – free association.

Working-through   The process in therapy, called psychic work, which enables us to free ourselves from the grip of repetition. When we repress feelings associated with particular ideas or feelings, we expend psychic energy. If repression is lifted – through bringing into consciousness what was previously unconscious – energy is released and can be redirected. In the relationship with the therapist the client is able to re-experience attitudes previously felt towards parents, or significant others, and it is in this way that old responses can be understood and, if necessary, eliminated. Working-through makes it possible for us to discover ways of living that are not simply based on past experiences.

Select bibliography

Bowlby, J. (1979) *The Making and Breaking of Affectional Bonds*, London: Tavistock.

Casement, P. (1985) *On Learning from the Patient*, London: Routledge.

—— (1990) *Further Learning from the Patient*, London: Routledge.

Davis, M. and Wallbridge, D. (1981) *Boundary and Space: An Introduction to the Work of D.W. Winnicott*, Harmondsworth: Penguin.

Freud, S. (1984) *The Theory of Psychoanalysis*, vol. 11, *On Metapsychology*, Harmondsworth: Penguin Books.

Langs, R. J. (1976) *The Technique of Psychoanalytic Psychotherapy*, vol. 1, New York: Jason Aronson.

—— (1978) *The Listening Process*, New York: Jason Aronson.

—— (1988) *A Primer of Psychotherapy*, New York: Jason Aronson.

Laplanche, J. and Pontalis, J.B. (1973) *The Language of Psychoanalysis*, London: Hogarth Press.

Livingston Smith, D. (1991) *Hidden Conversations*, London: Tavistock/Routledge.

Milner, M. (1952) 'Aspects of symbolism and comprehension of the not-self', *International Journal of Psychoanalysis* 33: 181–95.

Rawls, J. (1970) 'Two concepts of rules', in P. Foot (ed.), *Theories of Ethics*, Oxford: Oxford University Press.

Rogers, C. (1965) *Client Centred Therapy*, London: Constable.

—— (1974) *On Becoming a Person*, London: Constable.

Searles, H. (1975) *The Patient as Therapist to his Analyst: The Basis of the Psychoanalytic Process*, London: George Allen & Unwin.

Suggested reading

This list includes books concerned just with theory, books about theory and practice, two dictionaries, as well as some fictional works. The latter are given either because they describe childhood experiences, or because they give us insight into the human predicament.

Axline, V. (1971) *Dibs: In Search of Self*, Harmondsworth: Penguin.
Balint, M. (1952) *The Basic Fault*, London: Tavistock.
Bowlby, J. (1979) *The Making and Breaking of Affectional Bonds*, London: Tavistock.
Bollas, C. (1987) *The Shadow of the Object: Psychoanalysis of the Unknown Thought*, London: Free Association Books.
Boy, A. and Pine, G. (1982) *Client Centred Counselling – A Renewal*, Allyn and Bacon.
Casement, P. (1985) *On Learning from the Patient*, London: Tavistock/ Routledge.
—— (1990) *Further Learning from the Patient*, London: Routledge.
Davis, M. and Wallbridge, D. (1981) *Boundary and Space – an Introduction to the Work of D.W. Winnicott*, Harmondsworth: Penguin.
Dickens, C. (1985) *David Copperfield*, Harmondsworth: Penguin.
Erikson, E. (1951) *Childhood and Society*, London: Paladin.
Freud, S. (1977) *Case Histories I: 'Dora' and 'Little Hans'*, vol. 8, Pelican Freud Library, Harmondsworth: Penguin.
—— (1979) *Case Histories II: 'Rat Man', Schreber, 'Wolf Man'*, vol. 9, Pelican Freud Library, Harmondsworth: Penguin.
Fromm, E. (1960) *The Fear of Freedom*, London: Routledge & Kegan Paul.
Hinshelwood, R. D. (1989) *A Dictionary of Kleinian Thought*, London: Free Association Books.
Jacobs, M. (1988) *Psychodynamic Counselling in Action*, London: Sage.
Kohut, H. (1971) *The Analysis of the Self*, New York: International Universities Press.
Kubler-Ross, E. (1970) *On Death and Dying*, London: Tavistock.
Laing, R.D. (1970) *The Divided Self*, Harmondsworth: Penguin.
Laplanche, J. and Pontalis, J.B. (1973) *The Language of Psychoanalysis*, London: Hogarth Press.

Malan, D.H. (1980) *Individual Psychotherapy and the Science of Psychodynamics*, London: Butterworth.

Mearns, D. and Thorne, B. (1988) *Person-Centred Counselling in Action*, London: Sage.

Pincus, L. and Dare, C. (1978) *Secrets in the Family*, London: Faber & Faber.

Rogers, C. (1965) *Client Centred Therapy*, London: Constable.

—— (1974) *On Becoming a Person*, London: Constable.

Salinger, J. D. (1977) *The Catcher in the Rye*, London: Bantam.

Searles,H. (1986) *My Work with Borderline Patients*, New York: Jason Aronson.

Segal, H. (1975) *Introduction to Melanie Klein*, London: Hogarth.

Skynner, R. (1976) *One Flesh, Separate Persons*, London: Constable.

Skynner, R. and Cleese, J. (1983) *Families and How to Survive Them*, London: Methuen.

Sophocles (1981) *The Theban Plays*, Harmondsworth: Penguin.

Symington, N. (1986) *The Analytic Experience*, London: Free Association Books.

Tolstoy, L. (1989) *Anna Karenina*, London: Oxford University Press.

Winnicott, D.W. (1971) *Playing and Reality*, Harmondsworth: Penguin.

Index